More praise for *The Optimistic Leftist:*

"Progressives could use a dose of optimism, and Teixeira makes a strong case for it. While the U.S. electorate pulled the lever for the politics of fear, he argues that a coherent, forward-looking, inclusive agenda for strong, equitable growth will ultimately prove a winner. As Democrats regroup in the wake of an election that left the Republican Party in control of the federal and most state governments, they would do well to consider his thoughtful approach."   —Heather Boushey, author of

Finding Time: The Economics of Work-Life Conflict

"Trump's election has only intensified the American left's pessimism— a lack of faith in its ideals, solutions, and its ability to win over the American public. Ironically, as Ruy Teixeira shows, not only is that pessimism unwarranted, it is ultimately counterproductive to achieving liberal victory."

—Markos Moulitsas, founder and publisher of Daily Kos

"Ruy Teixeira's specialty is taking the long view when others are bound up in the next news or election cycle. In *The Optimistic Leftist,* he advances an analysis that should encourage progressives, be cautionary for conservatives, and engage and enlighten everyone who cares about America's political and economic future."

—James Fallows, national correspondent, *The Atlantic*

"This engaging and highly readable book will do much to lift the spirits of progressives who were disappointed by the results of 2016 Presidential election. Taking the long view, Ruy Teixeira makes a compelling case that a variety of macro forces—demographic, economic and social—will enable a leftist agenda to prevail for much of the 21st century."

—William H. Frey, Brookings Institution, and author of
Diversity Explosion: How New Racial Demographics Are Remaking America

"Ruy Teixeira is one of America's smartest and most far-seeing social observers. He has a rare ability to carefully consider opposing perspectives, without being trapped by the conventional wisdom, and arrive at pointed and even shocking conclusions that are later vindicated. His argument is one liberals ought to heed."

—Jonathan Chait, author of *Audacity: How Barack Obama Defied
His Critics and Transformed America*

"Essential reading for perspective and political balance in this dark age of nationalist populism, growing international disorder, and ongoing corporate plunder."

—Joel Rogers, co-author of *Right Turn: The Decline of the
Democrats and the Future of American Politics*

"Ruy Teixeira shows leftists and centrists, cosmopolitans and communitarians, organizers and activists the way to a pragmatic utopianism based on the energy and accomplishments of humanity."

—J. Bradford DeLong, professor of economics, U.C. Berkeley

THE

OPTIMISTIC

LEFTIST

Why the 21st Century Will Be
Better Than You Think

RUY TEIXEIRA

St. Martin's Press   New York

www.stmartins.com

Cataloging-in-Publication Data is available from the Library of Congress.

Hardcover ISBN 9781250089663
e-book ISBN 9781250089670

Our books may be purchased in bulk for promotional, educational, or business use. Please contact your local bookseller or the Macmillan Corporate and Premium Sales Department at 1-800-221-7945, extension 5442, or by e-mail at MacmillanSpecialMarkets@macmillan.com.

First Edition: March 2017

10 9 8 7 6 5 4 3 2 1

For the broad left and the struggle for a better future.
Oh, and by the way, cheer up!

TABLE OF CONTENTS

Against Pessimism

On November 8, 2016, Donald Trump was elected president of the United States. To say this was a shock to the political system is a considerable understatement.

It has never been more important to take a long view of the left's future and not dwell on short-term setbacks. A key effect of Trump's election is the beginning of the end for austerity economics, formerly the linchpin of conservative policy. Trump's professed commitment to massive spending on infrastructure and his ostentatious lack of interest in deficit reduction is blowing a hole in austerity dogma that should be welcomed by the left. The decline in that dogma will finally make it possible to break out of the "low growth trap" that has bedeviled the United States and other advanced countries.

Over time, this development will make all the priorities of the left much easier to move forward. The right will continue to be divided between proponents and opponents of austerity, while the left will unite around policies that promote more and better economic growth. But to succeed the left must proceed with confidence and, yes, optimism.

Granted, the words "optimism" and "the left" do not seem to go together very well these days. The dominant view on the left—reinforced by Trump's victory—is as follows: (1) progress in today's world has largely stopped and in many ways reversed; (2) the left is weak and at the mercy of a rapacious capitalism and a marauding right; and (3) the outlook for the future is bleak, with ordinary citizens suffering even more deprivation and the planet itself sliding inexorably toward catastrophe.

Over the years I have argued formally and informally against each of these propositions. It is not the case that progress has stopped. Today, we live in a freer, more democratic, less violent and more prosperous world than we ever have before.

It is not the case that the left is at the mercy of the right. The form of the left is changing but its numbers are strong and growing. It remains a vital force—*the* vital force—for reforming capitalism.

And it is not the case that the future of humanity is

bleak. The problems we face today are solvable and, moreover, are likely to be solved in the coming decades. Life for ordinary citizens should improve dramatically over the course of the twenty-first century.

Making the case against these pessimistic propositions would be a good enough reason to write this book. But there is an additional reason that motivates me. It is the staggeringly obvious—at least to me—fact that pessimism dramatically undermines the appeal of the left. Why on earth would anyone sign up with a movement that believes the situation is so hopeless? What's so inspiring about that?

Nothing. Yet the left persists in promoting a viewpoint that leads to paralysis and inaction rather than robust action and positive change.

The left wasn't always like this. Historically, the left has been identified with a belief in the future and the feasibility of dramatic improvements in human welfare. That is how I saw it when I was growing up in the 1950s and 1960s and I was happy to join.

But something went wrong in the 1970s. The great hopes of the 1960s went aground on the harsh realities of stagflation and then rising inequality and a resurgent right. It was indisputable that progress in important ways was slowing down rather than speeding up as most on the left had hoped.

Various significant electoral defeats for the left followed—most famously the rise of Reagan in America and Thatcher in the UK. And anti-government ideology thrived, both in politics and economics. The idea that government was the problem, not the solution, gained political credibility that would have seemed unimaginable in previous decades, and economics became dominated by theories that glorified the results of the untrammeled market.

If that wasn't bad enough, new threats like global warming emerged that cast doubt on the future of humanity writ large. Scientific progress, which once spurred visions of flying cars and lives of abundance and leisure, now seemed powerless to stop the apocalypse (if not complicit in bringing it on).

On the left, optimism went out of fashion, where it has remained to this day. Instead, the left concentrated on reminding voters just how terrible things were becoming. And there was certainly a lot of plausible material along these lines, as Western capitalism continued to underperform in terms of both growth and the distribution of benefits from growth. Data has accumulated over time documenting this poor performance—particularly in the early twenty-first century and in the aftermath of the Great Financial Crisis—and has been duly promulgated by the left.

Even the great victories of the left in the social realm tended to get lost in this litany of despair. Not to mention concrete policy victories such as those secured by President Obama. In short, when the left was winning, it often acted as if it was losing. Not surprisingly, the desired surge in left support has not materialized.

It is time to recognize that pessimism convinces no one. Marx was wrong about the immiseration of the proletariat, and contemporary leftists are wrong about the immiseration of the middle class. What is correct is that progress has slowed down, not that it has stopped or reversed. What is correct is that people want to move up from their current life, not that they believe there is nothing good about their current life. What is correct is that pessimism makes people less likely to believe in positive change, not more likely.

Finally, what is correct is that the best tonic for the left will be the return of solid and better-distributed economic growth, not just the continuing documentation of our current poor performance. Such growth is eminently possible even without a "political revolution." Good economic times will promote upward mobility and a sense of personal optimism. That optimism, in turn, will promote a climate of social generosity, tolerance and orientation toward collective advance that will greatly facilitate the agenda of the broad left.

That has been generally true throughout history and recent history indicates that it is still true today. It is time for the left to realize that its romance with pessimism is a bug not a feature of its current practice. There are no substitutes for optimism and an economic climate that promotes optimism. This seemingly simple but overlooked truth is why I wrote this book.

THE
OPTIMISTIC LEFTIST

Welcoming the Future

The left is likely to dominate the twenty-first century and there is little the right can do about this except adapt. This seems counter-intuitive in light of the modest success the left has enjoyed since the Great Financial Crisis of 2008–09. Even in the United States, where Democrats held the presidency under Barack Obama for eight years, progressives have had difficulty moving their policies forward, suffering instead through an endless series of political battles with a determined and extreme Republican Party. This situation has only been exacerbated by the stunning election of Donald Trump to the presidency in 2016.

But this is a short-sighted perspective. It overemphasizes

the role of crisis and underestimates the role of long-term fundamental change. A look at the structural and economic shifts remaking advanced societies shows that the left is in a far better position to advance its agenda than the right. The twenty-first century, despite a rocky start, is likely to be a progressive century, in which the right will be forced to play on the left's terms to be competitive.

Here's why. Start with the rise of new postindustrial progressive coalitions across the advanced world. They are taking the place of coalitions based on the declining traditional or blue-collar working class. In the United States, the blue-collar workforce is down to only about a fifth of the total workforce. Closely related to this trend, employment in the industrial sector has dropped rapidly across countries, replaced by employment in the service sector. The current level of industrial employment in the United States is only 16 percent. In addition, as the ranks of the traditional working class have thinned they have also become generally less supportive of mainstream left parties. In the United States, the white working class, which contains the bulk of the traditional working class, has declined so much in its Democratic sympathies that it is now more accurately thought of as a Republican group.

Many observers on the left have despaired at these trends, concluding that the left in the twenty-first century is doomed. But the decline of the traditional working class is intimately bound up with a change that fundamentally favors the left: the broad structural shift away from manufacturing and toward a postindustrial, knowledge-based society embedded in a global economy. Accompanying this shift have been changes in family and values norms—lowered fertility, diversity in family forms, rise of post-material values, decline of traditional religion—sometimes referred to as the Second Demographic Transition. Together these changes have given rise to an explosion of left-leaning groups that is overshadowing the decline of the working class and powering the emergence of new left coalitions. Conservatives, in contrast, are relying ever more heavily on declining social sectors to buoy their electoral fortunes.

But if there is such potential for new progressive majorities, why is there such difficulty turning this demographic dividend into consistent progressive governance? Even in the United States, where the new coalition has been relatively united and successful, Barack Obama's two presidential victories were followed by routs in the Congressional elections of 2010 and 2014 and, in 2016, the election of Donald Trump to the presidency.

In Europe, while there have been some notable election victories for the left (e.g., France, Italy), the momentum from these victories has dissipated quickly. Across the continent, the left has lacked sufficient strength to carry its program forward and, even when in control of the government, has typically settled for a "responsible" administration of austerity that preserves as much as possible of the welfare state. This has made many social democratic parties increasingly unpopular. It would appear that the left's ability to move European societies onto a progressive path and keep them there faces severe limits at the current time.

But these political difficulties are not insuperable. In fact, they are highly likely to be overcome, for three reasons. The first reason is that rising coalitions will continue to grow, strengthening the left, while the right's base constituencies will continue to decline. Electoral arithmetic is therefore on the left's side.

The second reason is that only the left is willing to confront capitalism's "Piketty problem." The Piketty problem, as Thomas Piketty's magisterial *Capital in the 21st Century* establishes, is that capitalism has innate tendencies toward rising inequality and concentration of wealth that will increasingly crimp living standards and frustrate economic mobility in a slow growth environment. The left sees this as a real problem that cannot be solved by the market alone. The right is defined by its defense of market outcomes, no matter how dismal—hence its continuing support of counter-productive austerity measures. The right's view is out of touch with current and future economic reality and will be increasingly unpopular with voters.

The third reason is that the left will be forced to actually solve the Piketty problem. The solution to the Piketty problem is clear: government action to promote faster and more equitably distributed growth. The right has no interest in this; the left is intrinsically inclined in this direction even if support for this path has been less than robust in recent years, as parties fight a rearguard action to defend the welfare state. But electoral necessity will force them to move decisively in an activist direction. Their emerging constituencies—immigrants and minorities, professionals, the highly educated, women, singles, seculars, Millennials—by and large are not the chief beneficiaries of existing welfare states and need a twenty-first-century version of progressive state action to enable their future. The left's political future therefore lies in this new direction.

Call it the "opportunity state." Movement in this direction will be facilitated by two important factors. The first is the emergence of "middle-out" or "equitable growth" economics, a burgeoning school of economic thought which sees the economic health of the middle and aspirational classes as not just a desirable outcome of growth but rather as an actual driver—in fact, the key driver—of growth. Conversely, high inequality is seen as not just unfair and injurious to those who come out on the short end of the stick but as an active obstacle to growth.

This will allow the left to make a compelling case for building the opportunity state, arguing that strong growth is eminently possible and with a much fairer distribution of the spoils than we are currently seeing. Indeed, the latter is the precondition for the former. Thus, instead of plying the rich with tax cuts and other goodies on the trickle-down theory that the wealthy are the job creators, middle-out economics posits that a relentless focus on the economic health and dynamism of the middle and aspirational classes, the real job creators, is the correct way to grow the economy.

We can already see the outlines of this approach coming into being. Obama, Hillary Clinton and the mainstream of the Democratic Party have shifted away from their flirtation with deficit reduction and now embrace an economic philosophy that even Obama has termed "middle-out economics." Obama initially proposed, and candidate Clinton endorsed, an agenda that includes universal pre-K, free access to two-year colleges, paid family leave, subsidized child care and robust investment in infrastructure. Granted, most of this agenda has little chance of passage with the current Congress and presidency, but the Democrats are placing their bets that this is the agenda of the future.

Even in Europe we see signs that austerity's shelf life is limited. Indeed, there is little doubt that were not Germany and her institutional allies still using their economic muscle to prevent any loosening of austerity, Eurozone policy would have tilted toward fiscal expansion and growth long ago. It is highly unlikely that German chancellor Angela Merkel and company can keep the lid screwed down for much longer; the continued rise of left and right populist parties all over Europe, from Syriza in Greece and Podemos in Spain to the National Front in France and the Freedom Party in Austria, shows clearly that the situation is not stable. As the great economist Herbert Stein put it: "If something cannot go on forever, it will stop" (usually known as Stein's Law).

It is worth stressing just how little of substance the right-wing austerity offensive has managed to achieve, beyond stopping the economic recovery in Europe and delaying it in the United States. The welfare states in Europe have been starved of support but not fundamentally altered for the simple reason that they're too popular. And in the United States, the Affordable Care Act has passed and taken root, the Dodd-Frank financial regulations have been enacted, executive actions were taken to protect the environment and mitigate climate change and so on. The state has not been gutted; far from it, it is ready to be taken to another stage.

That new stage will be central to Democrats' identity by 2024 or so, and much of the debate between the parties will be about whether substantial government investment or a conservative alternative with a more limited, though still significant, role for government is more effective. For example, a Democratic presidential candidate in 2024 might be arguing for a dramatic expansion of the American educational system—ranging from universal pre-K through free college—while a Republican candidate might also advocate expanded access, but on a more limited basis, such as combining student subsidies with tax breaks for profit-making schools. Or Democrats might advocate a Manhattan Project–style massive investment in bringing down the price of clean energy and building the infrastructure to match, while Republicans might counter with more modest investments based on public-private partnerships. The debate, in short, will focus on *how* government can provide opportunity and growth for the middle and aspirational classes rather than *whether* government should try to do so.

The second factor facilitating movement toward the opportunity state is the tremendous potential of technological advance. Starting with the Industrial Revolution, periods of high growth have been driven by technological breakthroughs and the twenty-first century will be no different. We are still in the early days of the ICT (information and communications technology), biotechnology and renewable energy revolutions. Just as in the past, realizing the growth potential of these breakthroughs depends heavily on government support for advanced research, new infrastructure and higher levels of education. Since today's right is hostile to government action in all these areas, and even hostile to science itself in some instances, it will fail as a promoter of growth in the long term. The left, fundamentally pro-science and pro–support for technological change, will fill this void and reap the benefits of growth promotion.

This optimistic perspective is quite a contrast to the gloom and pessimism that currently pervades the left. Why is that? One reason is the Piketty problem discussed earlier. Capitalism has very real tendencies toward inequality which have been poorly resisted in the last several decades. That naturally makes the left feel like it is losing.

Another is the challenge to the welfare state and traditional left political parties since the 1970s. An era in which the welfare state expanded in a relatively unproblematic way and mass left political parties enjoyed great electoral success was succeeded by an era in which the welfare state has been on the defensive and left parties' electoral success has been mixed at best. Again, that makes many leftists feel like their cause is losing.

Still another is a sense on the left that some problems have been allowed to grow so large they can't be solved—that time is running out or has run out. Global warming is the best example of this, but the dominance of the one percent also qualifies, as do the rise of the robots, the struggles of the middle class and the fate of the poor. Hence, the feeling on the left of running hard but falling farther and farther behind what needs to be done.

Finally, there is the disappearance of a revolutionary alternative to capitalism. The revolution will not only "not be televised," as radical poet Gil Scott-Heron declared in 1970, it will not happen. And that's a good thing. Revolutions are highly risky endeavors, leading frequently to long-term economic disruption and authoritarianism. With the disappearance of socialism, the leading contender to replace capitalism, as a plausible systemic alternative, there seems little reason to run those risks. That's disappointing to many on the left who had hoped capitalism could be transcended in some form.

It's time for supporters of the left to fully acknowledge they are not capitalism's gravediggers, but rather its caretakers. Their job is to make capitalism work better, not to replace it. And, critically, as this book explains, they need to realize that their pessimism about the state of the world today and its future is deeply misguided. Instead, the twenty-first century, under the stewardship of the left, will likely be a century of both exceptional material progress and greater social justice. The era of the optimistic leftist is upon us; it is time for the left to discard its congenital pessimism and hop on board.

ONE

The Left in History—
How and Where Has the
Left Succeeded?

Before mapping out the left's future, it is first necessary to consider its past. This past, as we shall see, is widely misunderstood. When understood correctly, it helps bring the left's future into focus—a future far more promising than most currently believe.

What is the left? Historically, the term goes back to the French Revolution, when those who supported the absolute monarchy sat on the right in the National Assembly and those who supported change sat on the left. Through many changes and permutations, these terms have stayed with us to the present day, with similar, if updated, connotations.

The right today generally defends the class structure and economic outcomes of the current system (capitalism) as fair and efficient, sees traditional norms and social structures as fundamentally positive and does not believe that the scope of political and economic democracy needs to be expanded. The left generally believes the class structure and economic outcomes of the current system need to be significantly changed, sees traditional norms and social structures as negative constraints on human potential and does believe that the scope of political and economic democracy needs considerable expansion.

This is a pretty broad definition. But it is appropriate. There is no sound reason to confine one's definition of the left to those who believe capitalism is fatally flawed and must be replaced with something different or those who believe, more generally, that the current system must be radically restructured to achieve any modicum of justice. Socialists and radicals may choose to conceptualize themselves as "the left," categorizing those who believe significant reform within the system is both desirable and feasible as props to the system rather than part of the left. No one can stop them from doing so. But this is an arbitrary distinction we need not accept. Instead, the left should be defined on the basis of commitment to change, rather than on a single preferred strategy for achieving change.

Thus the left, broadly conceived, certainly includes socialists, social democrats and radicals, but also greens, liberals, progressives and generally left-of-center parties like the Italian and American Democrats. Defined in this way, how and where has the left succeeded historically? And by "success" I don't mean struggled valiantly or had large demonstrations: where have they actually achieved reforms that made people's lives better?

By and large, the left has achieved much more success when times were good than when times were bad. Hard economic times and rising inequality, rather than generating broad support for more democracy and social justice, more typically generate pessimism about the future and fear of change. In contrast, when times are good, when the economy is expanding and living standards are steadily rising for most of the population, people see better opportunities for themselves and are more inclined toward social generosity, tolerance and collective advance.

THE POST–CIVIL WAR ERA AND THE LEFT

Take, for example, the post–Civil War history of the United States until the Great Depression. The second industrial revolution gathered force right after the Civil War. A wave of technical innovation created or transformed the chemical, electrical, petroleum and steel industries. And massive infrastructure development knitted the country together into a powerful world-class economy. Growth was particularly strong in the 1870s: real per capita income went up almost 3 percent per year.[1]

Parallel to this economic advance, the first shoots of the

American welfare state came into being. Spending on poor relief in the states increased tenfold, and the postwar pension system for disabled veterans and veterans' wives—American's first national anti-poverty program—was dramatically expanded in 1879. Public spending on education ramped up all over the country.[2] And until the latter part of this period, significant progress was made on improving the condition of blacks, both legislatively and materially.

But this tremendous growth and climate of social advance did not last. Income growth in the post–Civil War era, which had started out so well, ran into severe problems in the 1880s. In that decade, per capita income growth fell to just 0.6 percent per year.[3] The situation worsened in the first half of the 1890s, as the recession of 1893 saw increased unemployment, from 4 percent to 18 percent, and sharply reduced incomes. By 1895, per capita income growth had stagnated for 15 years, punctuated by numerous economic dislocations, leading to bitter resentment among the working classes. The gap between the rich and poor—already a problem—worsened over this period,[4] with the wealthiest Americans amassing fabulous fortunes, while workers, particularly immigrant workers, lived in appalling conditions in the cities.

Then there were the farmers. This group was isolated from the urban-industrial life that was beginning to dominate the country, promoting a sense of relative economic decline and obsolescence. And with the declining farm prices initiated by the 1873 recession, they were suffering materially as well. By the end of that decade, wholesale farm prices had declined by 28 percent. By the mid-1890s, they had fallen another 43 percent. Between the early 1870s and the mid-1890s, the price of wheat fell from $1.12 a bushel to 50 cents or less, while the price of corn decreased from 48 cents a bushel to 21 cents a bushel.[5]

Finally, the rising "new middle class," especially its professional component, felt deeply aggrieved by the country's failure to make more progress. Despite the expert tools that were now at this class's disposal, there was little scope to apply those tools, as status quo interests fiercely resisted any kind of meliorative agenda. Thus, despite the fact that their economic situation was typically far better than the workers and farmers, their sense of frustration was as deep or deeper.

So by the time the 1890s rolled around, no one in America was really happy with the state of the country save the wealthy. Dissatisfaction was concentrated in three general areas: the evils of bigness, the evils of corruption and the evils of injustice. The concern with bigness was centered on the super-rich and the monopolies they controlled, which were believed to rig the economic game in their favor and impoverish the workers and farmers. The concern with corruption reflected the public's perception that the political parties were under the control of the big interests, who were using government to enrich themselves and fix elections, not to try to solve social problems. The concern with injustice included everything from the raw economic facts—workers' low wages and falling farm prices—to urban living conditions to racial oppression and the lack of women's suffrage. The solution, broadly speaking, was to break up and regulate bigness, reform government and elections to root out corruption and utilize expertise, and direct this reformed government toward the goal of social justice. The stage was set for a more progressive politics.[6]

The middle class had numerous organizations and projects working on various aspects of these problems in the 1880s and early 1890s. Included here would be movements for political reform in the cities, for helping the poor (e.g., Hull House in Chicago) and for women's suffrage. And workers did have some success in self-organization through union leader Terence Powderly's Knights of Labor, which peaked at 700,000 members in 1886. But first out of the gate in terms of real political impact were the farmers. Starting with the Grange movement, then the Alliances and finally an actual political party, the People's (Populist) Party, organized farmers pressed an ambitious reform agenda focused on limiting the power of big banks, brokers and merchants and reforming government to make it more democratic. The Omaha Platform adopted at the People's Party convention in 1892 called for the abolition of national banks, a graduated income tax, direct election of senators, civil service reform, a working day of eight hours, and government control of all railroads, telegraphs and telephones. It also called for replacing the gold standard with free coinage of silver, a provision designed to combat the deflation of farm prices and make it easier for farmers to repay their debts.

In the election of 1892, the People's Party did well—extremely well for a third party in America. They pulled over a million votes, 8 percent of the total, and carried five states: Kansas, North Dakota, Colorado, Idaho and Nevada. This strong showing raised the political profile of serious reform. But the party itself would not last long, due to the embrace of their free silver idea (though little else) by the Democrats under William Jennings Bryan in 1896. This led the People's Party to make Bryan their presidential candidate as well and essentially ended their role as an independent political force.

The result was a disaster for both the Democrats and the Populists. Both parties were indelibly identified with the economic interests of the farmers in the countryside that, in this case, were in direct conflict with the economic interests of the workers in the cities. Free silver would certainly help the farmers but workers would wind up with paychecks that bought less, thereby lowering their standard of living. Moreover, William McKinley and the Republicans defended high protective tariffs, while the Democrats/Populists opposed them. Again, this counterposed the interests of workers in the cities, who benefited from protection of the industries in which they worked, to those of farmers in the countryside.

In short, the election of 1896, despite Bryan's efforts to invoke a coalition of the "toiling masses" in the cities and countryside, pitted the interests of a declining class, the farmers, against those of a rising class, the urban workers. Moreover, Bryan's impassioned pleas were to voters who had experienced 15 years of stagnant living standards. This meant that, despite the very real discontent, voters were too fearful and unsettled to support a bold reform agenda.

All this was a recipe for defeat and defeat duly followed, driven by uniformly sharp Democratic losses in urban areas like Boston (19 percentage points), Baltimore (19 points), New York (17 points) and Philadelphia (16 points).[7] While some of this vote would come back to the Democrats in future presidential elections—and remain there for many state and local elections—the Republican claim on a significant share of the urban working-class vote would remain.

THE PROGRESSIVE ERA

But if the Populists were dead and Republicans ascendant, progressive reformers were still very much alive—in fact, they were just beginning a period of tremendous success. There were several reasons for this.

First, very little progress had actually been made in addressing the evils of bigness, corruption and social injustice—as indeed is generally the case when times are bad. Despite the efforts of Populists and reform activists, not much had changed since 1880. There were a few exceptions—the secret ballot had become widespread and a number of state legislatures had passed safety and workers' compensation laws. But this was very small beer compared to the problems progressive reformers were trying to remedy. So their agenda was, if anything, more relevant than ever.

Second, a key effect of the realigning election of 1896 was that reform sentiment was spread more uniformly across the two parties—a paradox, since the common interpretation at the time was that conservative Republicans had overcome radical Democrats. Ex-Republican urban reformers, or "Mugwumps," who had joined the Democrats in the 1880s, returned to their original party and promoted successful reform mayors like Hazen Pingree of Detroit and Golden Rule Jones of Toledo. Ex-Republican agrarian reformers who had joined the Populist Party also returned in large numbers to their original party. These returned Populists joined forces with agrarian reformers who had never left the party to create an insurgent reformist strand of Republicanism in states like Wisconsin (Robert La Follette) and Iowa (Albert Cummins).

Third, and critically, McKinley's election ushered in an era of strong economic growth that benefited all classes. Poor harvests in Europe increased demand for American farm products, while the availability of gold suddenly increased (Alaska and Yukon gold rushes, increased production from South Africa), loosening credit and the money supply. That eliminated the deflation problem that had

particularly bedeviled the farmers, while American industry was boosted by the rise of mass production in sectors like auto and steel. As a result, the intense conflict
between free silver and tariff protection swiftly faded into
irrelevance. Between 1896 and 1913, the economy more
than doubled in size and real per capita income rose by
2.5 percent per year.[8] Unemployment, which was still
14 percent in 1896, fell to 4 percent by 1901 and stayed
near that level until World War I, when it fell even lower.[9]
Manufacturing workers did particularly well, with their annual earnings rising steadily, including a spurt from $550
to $900 between 1908 and 1917.[10]

This concatenation of factors produced an exceptionally favorable climate for progressive reform after 1896. A
far-reaching reform program had already been popularized. Reform now had a powerful presence within both
parties, in each case spreading far beyond the ranks of
middle-class activists, who were particularly exercised by
the corruption issue, to workers and farmers concerned
with social and economic justice. Indeed, even within the
Democratic Party, where ethnic, working class–based "boss-
ism" had played such a central role, reformers like Al Smith
and Robert F. Wagner of New York and David Walsh of
Massachusetts emerged and played prominent roles. And
the improved economic situation ended the conflict over
free silver, which had divided workers and farmers and
diverted political energy from the central parts of the reform program. This prosperity also, as we would expect,

toned down nativist and other intolerant, backward-looking sentiments that always lurked at the edges of populism and promoted an optimistic orientation toward change and the common good.

In McKinley's first term, most of the reform victories were at the state and municipal level. While these victories were gratifying, reformers nevertheless felt frustrated because they knew many of their most important issues could only be addressed at the national level. But with McKinley's death through assassination in 1901 and his succession by Teddy Roosevelt, reform suddenly had the national-level advocate it needed.

In Roosevelt's first term, he moved cautiously, looking toward 1904, when he could be elected president in his own right. But he did move to establish the power of the federal government to expose and act upon monopolistic corporate practices. In 1902, he initiated a suit against a new and powerful railroad combination, the Northern Securities Company. And while the traditional Republican approach had been to favor capital, Roosevelt moved to make government more of an impartial regulator of labor and capital. In the 1902 United Mine Workers (UMW) strike, he actually threatened to seize the mines if employers did not agree to impartial federal arbitration. Eventually, the UMW won a nine-hour day and a 10 percent wage increase. It was no coincidence that such labor victories took place in this era and not during the hard times that preceded the election of 1896.

Roosevelt promised a "Square Deal" for everyone in the 1904 campaign and won re-election with a thumping 57 percent of the vote, losing no states outside the south. He then proceeded to move more authoritatively in a reform direction. In 1906, the Hepburn Railroad Regulation Act was passed, giving the Interstate Commerce Commission—whose purview had been strictly limited by the courts—the right to inspect the books of railroad companies. Also in 1906, the Pure Food and Drug and Meat Inspection Acts were passed, getting the federal government into the business of protecting the people's health. In 1907, he proposed even bolder reforms, including the eight-hour day, broader worker compensation, inheritance and income taxes, and regulation of the stock market. He also vastly expanded the national forest system to take millions of acres out of private development hands.

Roosevelt had promised not to serve more than two terms and did in fact face serious opposition from conservatives in his own party who were outraged by his "radical" actions and rhetoric as president. He elected not to run for president in 1908 and instead designated his hand-picked successor, William Howard Taft, to carry on the progressive cause as the Republican nominee. Taft ran as a reformer, even adding some of his opponent William Jennings Bryan's reform ideas to the portfolio he inherited from Roosevelt.

Taft easily won the 1908 election with roughly the same coalition that elected Roosevelt in 1904, albeit with a somewhat lower vote total. However, once Taft assumed office it became apparent that his reform commitments were considerably tempered by attentiveness to business interests. He failed to meaningfully lower protective tariffs, which reformers increasingly believed was essential to undermining the power of the trusts. He also removed Roosevelt's conservationist secretary of the interior, James Garfield, replacing him with Richard Ballinger, a corporate lawyer. Ballinger promptly attempted to make a million acres of public lands available for private development.

These and other actions infuriated the reform wing of the Republican Party, which ran insurgent candidates against conservatives in party primaries in 1910. The reform Republican candidates defeated many of their opponents, while suffering no losses of their own. Democrats hopped on the reform bandwagon as well, running progressive candidates of their own. They succeeded in taking control of the House of Representatives for the first time in 16 years and made significant gains in the Senate. The electorate was clearly ready for further and bolder reforms.

Taft was not impervious to these sentiments and attempted on other fronts to prove his reformist bona fides. He was active on the trust-busting front, prosecuting 80 lawsuits against the trusts. He also further strengthened the Interstate Commerce Commission, reformed the postal system and expanded the civil service. And, though these amendments did not pass until Woodrow Wilson's administration, Taft supported both the 16th Amendment (allowing a federal income tax) and the 17th Amendment (direct election of senators by voters to replace selection by state legislatures).

Nevertheless, these moves were not enough to appease Republican progressives and he wound up facing challenges for the 1912 Republican nomination. First this came from Robert La Follette but then more consequentially from Roosevelt himself, who returned to active politics in September 1910 with his famous "New Nationalism" speech in Osawatomie, Kansas. Roosevelt argued that only a strong federal government could effectively pursue social justice and promote the common good. He supported, among other things, progressive income and inheritance taxes, child labor laws, workers' compensation for industrial accidents and tougher regulation of corporations.

But Taft would not yield to Roosevelt's challenge and the Republican Party split in two for the 1912 election. The progressives formed a new party, the Progressive Party, with Roosevelt as their candidate and the conservative Republicans renominated Taft. Rounding out the field were Woodrow Wilson for the Democrats and Eugene Debs for the Socialists.

The Progressive Party brought together numerous social reformers, activists and political insurgents under an expansive banner of national political change. Arguing that the country had reached the pinnacle of progressive sentiment, the Progressive Party put forth its "contract with the people" to help eliminate the "hazards of sickness, accident, invalidism, involuntary unemployment and old age."[11]

Wilson's candidacy for the Democrats was hugely significant since it was the first time a truly progressive, as opposed to populist, reformer had been nominated by the Democrats. The Democrats' New Freedom platform of 1912 had much in common with the New Nationalism approach of Roosevelt, differing primarily in approaches to trusts and economic concentration: Roosevelt wanted aggressive regulation of the trusts, while Wilson argued that breaking up the trusts, rather than regulating them, was the real solution.

Taken together then, the voters in 1912 had three progressive candidates (including Debs) to choose from and one conservative candidate. The result was a landslide for progressivism. Three of every four votes cast was for Wilson, Roosevelt or Debs. Taft received a meager 23 percent of the vote, carrying only the states of Utah and Vermont. Roosevelt carried 27 percent of the vote and the states of Pennsylvania, Michigan, Wisconsin, South Dakota, California and Washington. But Wilson's 42 percent plurality sufficed to carry every other state, giving him an overwhelming 435 electoral votes.

The 1912 progressive vote, while spread across three different candidates, prefigured the progressive coalition that would come to dominate the country in the New Deal era. Perhaps for the first time, the rising working class was completely in the progressive camp, along with the urban middle class and significant sections of the farmers. The future for progressivism, in the midst of the long boom of the early twentieth century, seemed full of promise.

And in many ways, the Wilson era delivered on that promise. In 1913, the 16th (allowing income taxes) and 17th (direct election of senators) Amendments finally were ratified by enough states, thanks to the unstinting efforts of progressives. Wilson followed up on the 16th Amendment by getting Congress to pass a progressive federal income tax. Also in 1913, he succeeded in reforming the banking sector through the Federal Reserve Act, which created a system of twelve regional banks to manage and stabilize banking activity. In 1914, he proposed and Congress passed the Federal Trade Commission Act, creating a federal agency with considerable regulatory power to police business. Interestingly, this latter idea was originally proposed by Roosevelt and was more characteristic of his New Nationalism approach than Wilson's New Freedom approach.

Later on in Wilson's presidency, he appointed progressive Louis Brandeis to the Supreme Court in 1916. Brandeis was the first Jew to serve on the Court. Wilson also supported a measure creating a system of workers' compensation for federal employees and another measure, the Keating-Owen Act, the first federal law regulating child labor. When the latter law was struck down by the Supreme Court, he had another law passed that heavily taxed products using child labor.

However, Wilson was not so friendly to other progressive reform efforts, refusing, for example, to support the ongoing drive for women's suffrage. (Despite his lack of support, the 19th Amendment, giving women the vote, was finally ratified by enough states in 1920.) And shamefully he supported legal segregation in federal agencies, reversing much of the work Roosevelt had done to eliminate racial barriers.

He also did little that could keep the progressive movement going once his presidency was over. In his second term, he became preoccupied with international affairs due to the U.S. entry into World War I. And he played a central role in promoting the Red Scare of 1917–20, where domestic radicalism became a target of both police suppression and nativist sentiment. The resulting atmosphere was hardly conducive to the cause of progressive reform.

THE FADING OF THE PROGRESSIVE ERA

To some extent, the progressive movement was also a victim of its own success. By 1920, progressives had had dramatic success breaking up corrupt political machines in the cities, promoting the use of nonpartisan technical experts (e.g., city managers) and expanding democracy in the states through initiatives, referenda and recall. And much of their reform agenda had been implemented: direct election of senators, a progressive federal income tax, much tougher regulation of business, lowering of protective tariffs, women's suffrage, action against child labor, federal regulation of food safety, a workmen's compensation law, civil service reform and a stable banking system that was fair to the South and the West.

Finally, and critically, the national spirit of optimism that buoyed the progressives during most of the Progressive Era withered in the face of economic problems that set in soon after the end of World War I. America suffered four separate recessions between 1918 and 1927, with a particularly sharp one in 1920–21, and a fifth, which initiated the Great Depression, in 1929. By 1921, price deflation had returned, affecting both industrial and farm prices. Indeed, economic conditions in the early postwar years were in many ways reminiscent of the difficult era of the 1880s and early 1890s.

However, the economy did recover after these early years, posting particularly strong growth in 1922–23, in 1926 and in 1929, right before the stock market crash. It is to these years, and to general trends like a surging stock market and a rising consumer economy, that we owe our image of the "Roaring Twenties" as an era of unmatched prosperity. In actuality, overall progress across the 1918–1929 period was considerably slower than in the Progressive Era (1.8 percent per year growth in per capita income,[12] compared to 2.5 percent per year in the earlier period), plus much of that progress was unevenly distributed. Income and wage inequality increased considerably,[13] and farmers and many workers outside of urban manufacturing did comparatively poorly.

As a result of all this, the progressive movement found itself adrift and, in remarkably short order, removed from national power. Conservative Warren Harding secured the Republican nomination in 1920, an indicator of the fading fortunes of progressives within the Republican Party. Harding ran on a promise to "Return to Normalcy," a slogan with nativist, isolationist and anti-progressive connotations. Harding's priorities were an accurate precursor of the politics of the 1920s, which saw a sharp increase in racial violence and the rise of the Ku Klux Klan, new restrictions on immigration, rises in protective tariffs, increases in economic concentration and tax cuts for the rich.

Harding easily defeated progressive Democrat James Cox for the presidency. Cox, in fact, received only 34 percent of the popular vote and carried no states outside of the South. As poorly as Cox fared, he did better than the Democrats' next presidential nominee, conservative corporate lawyer John Davis, in 1924. Davis received just 29 percent of the vote, carrying roughly the same states as Cox and losing handily to conservative Republican Calvin Coolidge, the incumbent (Coolidge had assumed the presidency upon Harding's death in 1923).

The Democrats' nomination of Davis also provided political space for progressives to run their own candidate in 1924, Robert La Follette, running on the same Progressive Party line Roosevelt did in 1912. La Follette did not do quite as well as Roosevelt, though very well indeed for a third-party presidential candidate. He received 17 percent of the vote, but carried only his home state of Wisconsin. He did relatively well in the northern states running from Wisconsin to the Pacific coast and in California. But he did relatively poorly in the east.

Other than La Follette's 1924 candidacy, the real progressive action in this period was in the states—for example, the rise of the Minnesota Farmer-Labor Party. State-level progressives kept the torch burning, seeking to build their strength for their next big opportunity. Their efforts bore some fruit in 1928, when Democrats, hoping to capitalize on discontent among urban workers and rural farmers, made progressive Al Smith their nominee.

Smith, a New York City born-and-bred Irish Catholic, was perhaps not perfectly suited to appeal to rural America, but he nevertheless made significant Democratic gains in these areas. For example, he carried 45 counties in Illinois, Iowa, Minnesota and North Dakota that had not been carried by any Democrat since Wilson.[14] Smith was well-suited, however, to increasing Democratic penetration of the urban working class, particularly in the northeast, regaining ground that Democrats had been struggling to hold ever since the McKinley election of 1896. His huge majority in Boston converted Republican Massachusetts into Democratic Massachusetts, which it remains to this day. He also turned Providence and the state of Rhode Island Democratic, as well as cities such as New Haven, Scranton, Wilkes-Barre and Albany, and expanded Democratic majorities in urban areas like New York City and Jersey City. In this sense, Smith's losing effort to conservative Republican Herbert Hoover, who carried 58 percent of the vote and 444 electoral votes, prefigured the far different electoral results of 1932, which will be discussed later in this chapter.

THE POSTWAR BOOM AND THE GREAT SOCIETY

The other great example from American history that fits the "good times help the left/bad times hurt the left" pattern is the post–World War II history of the country. World War II itself was a time of stunning economic dynamism in the United States: from 1941 to 1945 U.S. per capita income rose at over a 9 percent annual rate.[15] Of course, that wasn't sustainable, but even after the war the United States enjoyed almost 30 years of rapid economic advance.

Underpinning this era of advance was the adoption of the Keynesian economic consensus—a consensus that had evolved across the Western world in the late 1930s and during the world war. Following this consensus, U.S. progressives, who dominated Congress and the presidency for several decades after World War II, focused on managing economic demand, primarily through fiscal policy, to maintain full employment. Also following Keynesian precepts this activist fiscal policy included a big role for public investment. Returning GIs were provided with a free college education and low-interest, zero-down-payment home loans through the GI Bill. And government poured money into roads, science, public schools and whatever else seemed necessary to build up the country. Overall public investment by the federal government as a percent of GDP climbed steadily to around 2.6 percent of GDP per year by the end of the Keynesian era.[16] Core infrastructure investment (in transportation, energy, water management) increased particularly rapidly (4.3 percent per year from 1950 to 1974). [17]

The results of this economic regime were impressive. The GDP growth rate was 3.8 percent per year between 1946 and 1973, and the per capita GDP growth rate was 2.4 percent over the same period.[18] Unemployment, though considered high compared to booming Europe, averaged 4.8 percent over these years.[19] And the growth in living standards was phenomenal: real median family income rose at a rate of 2.8 percent per year, more than doubling over the time period.[20] Moreover, this income growth was remarkably equally distributed, with, if anything, a little stronger growth at the bottom and a little weaker growth at the top.[21]

Building upon this foundation of strong economic growth and rising incomes for the middle class and poor, progressives continued and refined the regulatory approach, social protections and economic security measures of the New Deal. And with Lyndon Johnson's Great Society reforms of the mid-60s, they dramatically expanded government action in all these areas.

Most fundamentally, they attacked the continued existence of racial discrimination and oppression. Johnson signed the Civil Rights Act in 1964 and the Voting Rights Act in 1965.

The continued existence of poverty, an issue popularized by Michael Harrington's 1962 book, *The Other America*, was addressed through the Economic Opportunity Act of 1964, which launched the "War on Poverty." The War on Poverty included such initiatives as the Job Corps, VISTA, the Model Cities program, Upward Bound and Project Head Start.

The health care woes of older Americans, which frequently impoverished them, were addressed through the creation of Medicare in 1965, a universal health care program for the elderly. In the same year, Medicaid was established to provide basic medical care for the poor.

Environmental issues were targeted by a wide range of new initiatives going far beyond the federal government's traditionally limited commitments in this area. The Clean Water, Water Quality and Clean Water Restoration Acts were passed. So too were the Wilderness Act, the Endangered Species Preservation Act, the Solid Waste Disposal Act and many others. The stage was set for creation of the Environmental Protection Agency (EPA) in 1970 and the activist environmental policies we are used to today.

Chronic money problems of low-income schools were addressed by getting the federal government into the education funding business through the Elementary and Secondary Education Act. Federal support for colleges and universities and for assistance to low-income students was increased through the Higher Education Act.

Consumer protection was enhanced through the Motor Vehicle Safety Act, the Fair Packaging and Labeling Act, the Child Safety Act, the Wholesome Meat and Poultry Acts and a number of other laws. These acts raised the bar for consumer protection far higher than it had previously been.

So, over nearly three decades, the Keynesian consensus in the United States produced strong economic growth, low unemployment, rapidly rising living standards and, through government, progressive actions to provide more protections and security for the average citizen. This produced a virtuous feedback loop between the political fortunes of progressives and the economic fortunes of the country.

Reflecting this feedback loop, until almost the very end of this period, the progressive-dominated Democratic Party received high levels of electoral support. As far as voters were concerned, progressives had delivered a better and ever-richer society and deserved that support. In the six elections between 1932 and 1948, Democratic presidential support averaged 55 percent. After the liberal Republican Dwight Eisenhower won two terms, in 1952 and 1956, the Democrats again averaged 55 percent presidential support in the 1960 and 1964 elections. And during almost all of this period, the Democrats controlled both houses of Congress.

THE FADING OF THE POSTWAR BOOM AND
THE DECLINE OF THE LEFT

But this feedback loop was broken in the 1970s, as the complications of a globalizing economy started to bite. These complications undermined the stable international economic relationships of the postwar Bretton Woods system, including fixed exchange rates. The *coup de grace* was administered by the OPEC oil price shock of 1973. Inflationary pressures that had been building up inside the United States and other advanced countries could no longer be contained, producing high inflation rates that could not be brought down by high unemployment. This combination of high unemployment with high inflation was termed "stagflation." Progressives at that time were unprepared with either an alternative to, or extension of, the postwar Keynesian system to fix this problem, which led to the end of the Keynesian consensus.

A conservative counter-revolution in economic thinking filled the vacuum left by the collapse of the Keynesian consensus. Conservatives, of course, had never been happy with the Keynesian consensus. Ideologically, they were opposed to the idea that the unregulated market had intrinsic flaws that only government could correct. And many conservatives had economic interests that predisposed them to resist and resent government intervention. So when the Keynesian system appeared to break down, they seized the opportunity to reinstate their views and discredit government's role. They succeeded beyond their wildest dreams.

Leading the charge was conservative economist Milton Friedman. In his academic work he showed how inflationary expectations could derail the Phillips curve (a well-behaved tradeoff between unemployment and inflation) favored by Keynesian economists. And, with his wife Rose, he published the enormously influential *Free to Choose*, a no-holds-barred polemic in favor of self-interested individuals making "rational," unregulated decisions and against anything that interfered with this process, especially government action. As far as Friedman was concerned, government's economic role should be limited to little more than controlling the growth of the money supply.

This economic philosophy was obviously no mere reform or adjustment of the Keynesian system but a complete turnaround—a true counter-revolution. In short order, it came to dominate economic policymaking in the United States and other advanced countries. Deregulation and privatization became the order of the day, while Keynesian fiscal policy, especially the central role of public investment, was shunted aside. In the United States, this led to significant deregulation of the transportation, energy, telecommunications and financial sectors. The latter included the repeal of the Glass-Steagall Act, a Depression-era law that mandated barriers between different kinds of financial firms so that, for example, a low-risk commercial bank could not also be a far higher-risk investment bank.

The results of the conservative economic regime have not been good. Indeed, in every important way it has produced economic results far inferior to those of the Keynesian era. Start with the slow growth in living standards for the typical family, accompanied by a remarkable rise in inequality. As mentioned earlier, the postwar era until 1973 was notable for equally distributed growth and a dramatic rise in living standards (nearly 3 percent per year growth in family income). From 1973 to 2014, growth in median family income averaged just 0.4 percent per year—an equally extraordinary slowdown—producing a mere 16 percent aggregate rise in incomes over a longer time period.[22]

Moreover, in a pattern economist Paul Krugman and others have termed the Great Divergence, income growth for the affluent and, even more so, for the rich has been far better than for the median family over the post-1973 period, while income growth for the poor has been worse. At the 80th percentile, family income rose by 41 percent and at the 95th percentile by 61 percent, but only by 4 percent at the 20th percentile.[23] In addition, income has become increasingly concentrated at the very highest reaches of the income distribution: the top 1 percent of the income distribution has been regularly receiving over one-fifth of total income in the last decade, most of which is received by the top one half of one percent.[24] These are levels of income concentration not seen in the United States since the 1920s.

The basic facts about the rise in inequality since 1973 are fairly well known. Less well known is how poorly the post-1973 period compares to the Keynesian era in terms of overall growth. In other words, it's not just that post-1973 growth has been poorly distributed; there's also been less of it. This fact is particularly damning for the conservative economics that replaced Keynesianism, because that economics was supposed to unshackle the great capitalist growth machine from the heavy hand of government. Instead, real GDP growth has actually slowed down: 2.7 percent per year in the post-1973 period, compared to 3.8 percent per year in the Keynesian era. A similar slowdown can be observed in GDP per capita growth, down to 1.7 percent per year from 2.4 percent.[25]

The conservative economic regime has been similarly unsuccessful in keeping down the unemployment rate. Despite encouraging the capitalist economy's allegedly natural tendency toward a full employment equilibrium, the conservative regime has produced higher average unemployment rates (6.1 percent) than those in the Keynesian era (4.8 percent).[26]

Accompanying this underwhelming record on living standards, inequality, growth and employment has been a steep decline in levels of public investment, considered of little importance by a conservative economics enraptured with the private sector. Overall public investment by the federal government as a percentage of GDP slipped from 2.6 percent per year at the end of the Keynesian era to 1.9 per year in the 2000s.[27] And core infrastructure (transportation, energy, water management) investment slowed dramatically, from a 4.3 percent per-year average growth rate in the 1950–74 period to just 2.3 percent per year in the 1975–2007 period.[28] Reflecting this neglect of infrastructure, the American Society of Civil Engineers has estimated that an additional $1.6 trillion in infrastructure investment is needed by 2020 simply to repair and maintain existing infrastructure in the United States, independent of any investments that might be needed to improve our current infrastructure (e.g., high-speed trains, broadband networks, and clean energy smart grids).[29]

Consistent with most of U.S. history, this run of relatively bad times has been generally bad for the left. And it has been most conspicuously bad in terms of support among the white working class. A sketch of the philosophy and politics of postwar U.S. progressives clarifies why this has been so. Postwar progressives' worldview was shaped by a combination of the Democrats' historic populist commitment to the average working American and their experience in fighting the Great Depression and World War II (and building their political coalition) through increased government spending and regulation and the promotion of labor unions. It was really a rather simple philosophy, even though its application was complex. Government should help the average person through vigorous government spending. Capitalism needs regulation to work properly. Labor unions are good. Putting money in the average person's pocket is more important than rarified worries about the quality of life. Traditional morality is to be respected, not challenged. Racism and the like are bad, but not so bad that the party should depart from its main mission of material uplift for the average American.

That worldview had deep roots in an economy dominated by mass production industries and was politically based among the workers, overwhelmingly white, in those industries. And it helped make the Democrats the undisputed party of the white working class. Their dominance among these voters was, in turn, the key to their political success.

To be sure, there were important divisions among these voters—by country of origin (German, Scandinavian, Eastern European, English, Irish, Italian, etc.), by religion (Protestants vs. Catholics), and by region (South vs. non-South)—that greatly complicated the politics of this group, but the New Deal progressives mastered these complications and maintained a deep base among these voters.

Of course, the New Deal coalition as originally forged did include most blacks and was certainly cross-class, especially among groups like Jews and southerners. But the prototypical member of the coalition was indeed an ethnic white worker—commonly visualized as working in a unionized factory, but also including those who weren't in unions or who toiled in other blue-collar settings (construction, transportation, etc.). It was these voters who powered four FDR election victories and the victories of Truman, Kennedy and Johnson, as well as the Democrats' Congressional domination.

So New Deal progressives depended on the white working class for political support and the white working class depended on progressives to run government and the economy in a way that kept that upward escalator to the middle class moving. Social and cultural issues were not particularly important to this mutually beneficial relationship; indeed they had only a peripheral role in the uncomplicated progressivism that animated the Democratic Party of the '30s, '40s and '50s. But that arrangement and that uncomplicated progressivism could not and did not survive the dynamic evolution of postwar capitalism.

On the one hand, this evolution changed the character of the white working class, reducing the size and influence of the Democrats' traditional blue-collar constituencies. On the other, the growth of postwar capitalism was creating new constituencies and movements with new demands. These new constituencies and movements wanted more out of the welfare state than steady economic growth, copious infrastructure spending and the opportunity to raise a family in the traditional manner.

During the sixties, these new demands on the welfare state came to a head. Americans' concern about their quality of life overflowed from the two-car garage to clean air and water and safe automobiles; from higher wages to government-guaranteed health care in old age; and from access to jobs to equal opportunities for men and women and blacks and whites. Out of these concerns came the environmental, consumer, civil rights and feminist movements of the Sixties. As Americans abandoned the older ideal of self-denial and the taboos that accompanied it, they embraced a libertarian ethic of personal life. Women asserted their sexual independence through the use of birth control pills and through exercising the right to have an abortion. Adolescents experimented with sex and courtship. Homosexuals "came out" and openly congregated in bars and neighborhoods.

Of these changes, the one with most far-reaching political effects was the civil rights movement and its demands for equality and economic progress for black America. Democratic progressives, both because of their traditional, if usually downplayed, anti-racist ideology and their political relationship to the black community, had no choice but to respond to those demands, as Lyndon Johnson finally did in 1964–65. The result was a great victory for social justice, but one that created huge political difficulties for the Democrats among their white working-class supporters. Kevin Phillips captured these developments well in his book *The Emerging Republican Majority*:

> The principal force which broke up the Democratic (New Deal) coalition is the Negro socioeconomic revolution and liberal Democratic ideological inability to cope with it. Democratic "Great Society" programs aligned that party with many Negro demands, but the party was unable to defuse the racial tension sundering the nation. The South, the West, and the Catholic sidewalks of New

York were the focus points of conservative opposition to the welfare liberalism of the federal government; however, the general opposition . . . came in large part from prospering Democrats who objected to Washington dissipating their tax dollars on programs which did them no good. The Democratic party fell victim to the ideological impetus of a liberalism which had carried it beyond programs taxing the few for the benefit of the many . . . to programs taxing the many on behalf of the few.[30]

But if race was the chief vehicle by which the New Deal coalition was torn apart, it was by no means the only one. White working-class voters also reacted poorly to the extremes with which the rest of the new social movements became identified. Feminism became identified with bra-burners, lesbians and hostility to the nuclear family; the antiwar movement with the appeasement of Third World radicals and the Soviet Union; the environmental movement with a Luddite opposition to economic growth; and the move toward more personal freedom with a complete abdication of personal responsibility.

Thus the progressive mainstream that dominated the Democratic Party was confronted with a challenge. The uncomplicated New Deal commitments to government spending, economic regulation and labor unions that had defined the party's progressivism for over 30 years suddenly provided little guidance for dealing with an explosion of potential new constituencies for the party. Their demands for equality, and for a better, as opposed to merely richer, life were starting to redefine what progressivism meant and the Democrats had to struggle to catch up. Progressive action more and more seemed to be outside the party in radical organizations like Students for a Democratic Society (SDS) and in the new social movements.

Initially, progressive Democrat politicians responded to these changes in the fashion of politicians since time immemorial: they sought to co-opt these new movements by absorbing many of their demands, while holding onto the party's basic ideology and style of governing. This was the first step away from the standard New Deal model of progressivism. Progressive Democrats of that era didn't change their fundamental commitment to the New Deal welfare state, but grafted on support for all the various new constituencies and their key demands. After Lyndon Johnson signed the Civil Rights Act in 1964, the party moved over the next eight years to give the women's, antiwar, consumers' and environmental movements prominent places within the party. This reflected both the politician's standard interest in capturing the votes of new constituencies *and* the ongoing expansion in the definition of what it meant to be a Democrat, particularly a progressive one.

But there was no guarantee, of course, that gains among these new constituencies wouldn't be more than counter-balanced by losses among the old constituency—the white working class—who had precious little interest in this expansion of what it meant to be a progressive and a

Democrat. And indeed that turned out to be the case with the nomination and disastrous defeat of George McGovern—an enthusiastic advocate of this new approach—in 1972. McGovern's commitment to the traditional Democratic welfare state was unmistakable. But so was his commitment to all the various social movements and constituencies that were reshaping the party, whose demands were enshrined in McGovern's campaign platform. That made it easy for the Nixon campaign to typecast McGovern as the candidate of "acid, amnesty and abortion." The white working class reacted accordingly and gave Nixon overwhelming support at the polls, casting 70 percent of their votes for the Republican candidate.[31]

Indeed, just how far the Democratic Party fell in the eyes of the white working class over this time period can be seen by comparing the average white working-class vote for the Democrats in 1960 and 1964 (55 percent) to their average vote for the Democrats in 1968 and 1972 (35 percent).[32] That's a drop of 20 points. The Democrats were the party of the white working class no longer.

With the sharp economic recession and Nixon scandals of 1973–74, the Democrats were able to develop enough political momentum to retake the White House in 1976, with Jimmy Carter's narrow defeat of Gerald Ford. But their political revival did not last long.

Not only did the Carter administration fail to do much to defuse white working-class hostility to the new social movements, especially the black liberation movement, but economic events—the stagflation of the late 1970s—conspired to make that hostility even sharper. Though stagflation (combined inflation and unemployment with slow economic growth) first appeared during the 1973–75 recession, it persisted during the Carter administration and was peaking on the eve of the 1980 election. As the economy slid once more into recession, the inflation rate in that year was 12.5 percent. Combined with an unemployment rate of 7.1 percent, it produced a "misery index" of nearly 20 percent.

The stagflation fed resentments about race—about high taxes for welfare (which was assumed to go primarily to minorities) and about affirmative action. But it also sowed doubts about Democrats' ability to manage the economy and made Republican and business explanations of stagflation—which blamed it on government regulation, high taxes and spending—more plausible. In 1978, the white backlash and doubts about Democratic economic policies had helped to fuel a nationwide tax revolt. In 1980, these factors reproduced the massive exodus of white working-class voters from the Democratic tickets first seen in 1968 and 1972. In the 1980 and 1984 elections, Ronald Reagan averaged 61 percent support among the white working class, compared to an average of 35 percent support for his Democratic opponents, Jimmy Carter and Walter Mondale.[33]

Democrats appeared powerless to stop this juggernaut, saddled as they were with a double-barreled progressivism that increasingly seemed like a dual liability. On the one hand they were committed to a model of the welfare state economy that no longer seemed to work, and, on the other, they were tied to a set of constituency groups whose priorities seemed alien to middle America. It seemed to many progressives that their cause was hopeless, especially after their preferred candidate, Walter Mondale, got blown away in the 1984 election, losing every state but Minnesota and the District of Columbia.

It would take a quarter of a century from that low point for progressives to rise again to a stronger position. A great deal of this was powered by the ongoing diminution of the white working class and the emergence of a new progressive coalition based on rising demographics (much more on this in the next chapter). In addition, the impressive victory of 2008 that elected Barack Obama to his first term and brought the new progressive coalition center-stage in U.S. politics was powered by the Great Recession of 2007–09.

All told, Obama's administration resulted in some impressive advances (see chapter 4 for a detailed discussion), the most important of which was the passage and implementation of the Affordable Care Act or "Obamacare." It is reasonable to see the Obama administration as the most progressive administration since the days of Lyndon Johnson. For all that, Obama's twin election victories did not usher in the progressive era many were hoping for. Resistance to further progressive measures and budgetary priorities was stiff in many parts of the country and progressives were routed in the two Congressional elections of 2010 and 2014, followed by Hillary Clinton's defeat in the 2016 presidential election.

This has puzzled many on the left who assumed that the discrediting of the conservative economic regime in the crisis of 2007–09 would result in a durable shift to the left in U.S. politics. Instead, as is consistent with most of U.S. history, the Great Recession and poor economic performance since then has bred not just a thirst for progressive advance but also considerable fear and uncertainty, which presents a barrier to such advance.

Why this chronic tendency to ignore the lessons of history? One reason is intrinsic to the nature of the left: those on the left tend to believe the class structure and economic outcomes of the current system need significant change to achieve social justice. Therefore, when the system's outcomes are particularly bad, as they have been in recent years, they believe their case for change is exceptionally strong and should convince more people.

THE NEW DEAL AND THE LEFT'S GREAT EXCEPTION

The most important reason, however, is the tendency of the left to focus on one particular period of U.S. history rather than the general pattern. That period of course is the New Deal. In this era, American capitalism was in a far deeper crisis than it has been in since, including the Great Recession of 2007–09. And yet, contrary to other periods of U.S. history, these deep economic difficulties birthed an era of far-reaching reform. Here is how that happened.

The campaign of 1932 was held against the backdrop of the Great Depression, with 24 percent unemployment. The Democrats turned to Franklin Delano Roosevelt (FDR) as their standard-bearer, a long-time progressive within the party who was governor of New York and had run for vice president on the 1920 Democratic ticket. FDR ran as a full-throated progressive who promised to use the tools of government to build from the bottom up and help the "forgotten man." For this emphasis he was tagged with the "class warrior" label by many, including his rival for the nomination, 1928 Democratic candidate Al Smith. For Smith and some others who considered themselves progressive, FDR was just going too far and verging on anti-business radicalism.

But that was not how the voters saw it. FDR was elected in a landslide with 57 percent of the vote to Hoover's 40 percent and carried every state save Pennsylvania, Delaware, Connecticut, Vermont, New Hampshire and Maine. This was the first appearance of what came to be known as the New Deal coalition, based around Democratic domination of the rising blue-collar working class (at the time two-and-a-half times as large as America's farmers and farmworkers), especially urban Catholic ethnics and especially in mass production industries. In addition, this coalition included groups like blacks and Jews, who suffered discrimination in addition to their own economic problems, and white southerners generally, who had a historical attachment to the Democratic Party.

With this coalition backing him and a dire situation confronting the country, FDR proceeded to launch a wave of reform that considerably expanded the role for government in regulating the economy and achieving social justice. This was consistent with the aims and philosophy of progressivism, but went beyond anything progressives had previously attempted. In the famous first "Hundred Days," the Civilian Conservation Corps was created to provide jobs, the Federal Emergency Relief Administration to provide urban income support and the Agricultural Adjustment Administration to provide farm price supports and mortgage refinancing. Substantial funds were appropriated for new jobs-creating public works programs, eventually evolving into the Works Progress Administration. The Emergency Banking Act was passed, reopening banks and instituting a bank inspection regime. The Glass-Steagall Act was also passed, strengthening bank safety, controlling speculation and creating the Federal Deposit Insurance Corporation, as was the Federal Securities Act, mandating full disclosure of financial information in stock sales.

In these first hundred days and thereafter, FDR was under strong pressure to move in this progressive direction and keep moving. This was not just from Congress itself, where progressive Democrats were in a mood to take decisive action, but also outside of Congress and, in some cases, outside of the major party structure. Father Coughlin of Michigan had a radio audience of ten million and was seeking to organize a National Union for Social Justice. Francis Townsend of California championed a radical pension plan, forming Townsend Clubs across the country. Also in California, Upton Sinclair ran for governor in 1934 on his EPIC (End Poverty in California) program. Then there was Huey Long in Louisiana and his Share Our Wealth movement, Floyd Olson of the Minnesota Farmer-Labor Party and the La Follettes in Wisconsin, who left the GOP in 1934, forming a state-level Progressive Party that swept the state. And perhaps most important of all, there were the labor unions, especially the insurgent industrial unions that eventually formed the Congress of Industrial Organizations (CIO). Their unstinting support for continuing and deepening the New Deal was crucial to the progress of reform.

With this pressure and deep economic difficulties to overcome, progressive advance continued for much of the 1930s. The Securities and Exchange Commission was formed to strengthen stock market regulation. The Tennessee Valley Authority and Rural Electrification Administration were established. The U.S. Housing Authority was created to provide housing for low-income families. The Food, Drug and Cosmetic Act was passed, the beginning of modern drug regulation. The Social Security system was established. Union organizing was encouraged through the Wagner Act and the establishment of the National Labor

Relations Board. And the Fair Labor Standards Act was passed, specifying the 40-hour regular work week, mandating time and a half for overtime, prohibiting most child labor and setting a minimum wage.

Clearly, a great deal was accomplished in the 1930s, a veritable makeover of U.S. capitalism, even though the economic situation was generally dismal—per capita income did not recover to its pre-Depression level until 1940 and double-digit unemployment continued until U.S. entry into World War II. (Note, however, that the years 1934–36, when some of the most important New Deal legislation—Social Security, the Wagner Act on collective bargaining and the Rural Electrification Administration—was passed, were years of exceptionally fast economic growth, with over 10 percent GDP growth per year.) This has suggested to many on the left ever since that terrible economic times are when the left can expect to make the most progress.

But this is a very misleading model to work with. The spate of social progress during the Great Depression decade was very much the exception to the historical rule. A crisis on that scale, where desperation is so widespread that no alternative to radical change seems viable, is very unlikely to be repeated. Nor should we wish that to happen. Desperate times do indeed sometimes make for desperate measures, but there is no guarantee those desperate measures will be particularly progressive (think Germany in the very same decade of the 1930s). Instead we should be grateful that the automatic stabilizers and institutional safeguards built into capitalism today pull us back from the brink of such an all-encompassing crisis.

So if the Great Depression was the Great Exception to the general pattern of left advance, it is now time to decisively reject the Great Mistake that has been fostered by the Great Exception. The Great Mistake sees great things just around the corner in bad times if only the right strategy to galvanize the suffering masses to action can be discovered. This is not realistic. The idea that progress will be limited as long as bad times persist is far closer to the mark.

EUROPE AND TODAY

The European experience fits this pattern well (though, in contrast to the United States, there is generally not a period that stands out as a Great Exception).[34] In the heyday of industrial capitalism, from around 1860 to World War I, rising living standards, reflected in generally high per capita growth rates, were associated with a raft of reforms in European countries' democratic processes, significant improvements in citizens' access to education and upward mobility, and the beginnings of welfare state programs and regulations. The interwar years in the 1920s and 1930s were considerably spottier, both in terms of economic performance and social advance, and the Great Depression, contrary to its effects in the United States, was a source of tragic outcomes for many European countries.

The great burst of progress was after World War II,

where the left took advantage of unprecedentedly high growth rates and rapidly rising living standards to build out the European welfare states and thoroughly democratize their societies. But of course, as growth slowed after 1973, rising inequality began to bite (though generally not as much as in the United States), and as improvement in living standards became sluggish, social advance in Europe has correspondingly slowed down, just as in the United States.

So the general lesson of whether bad economic times or good times are best for left advance should be clear. It is absolutely necessary to agitate for progress during bad times—to defend previous progressive gains, to push reforms forward when they are possible and, of course, to develop the organizational strength of the left. But the strategic imperative of bad times should be to prepare for good times and help make those good times happen. Only then is the agenda of the left likely to have the success progressives seek.

This insight is especially timely today. The crisis of capitalism of the early twenty-first century has not delivered the climate for progressive advance that so many in our country hoped for. But a new progressive coalition is rising whose interests can only be served by a new and healthy stage of capitalist growth. Getting to that stage is the necessary precursor to the next big spate of progressive reform.

The same point applies with even more force to Europe. Progressives have been on the defensive, by and large, since

the Great Recession ushered in an era of economic instability and slow growth (or no growth at all for some countries). Yet there too new progressive coalitions are emerging
that could advance far—indeed, will only advance far—
with a restoration of good times. These new progressive
coalitions are the subject of the next chapter.

TWO

The Postindustrial
Progressive Coalition

Broadly speaking, the progressive coalition for perhaps 150 years—but most robustly for the hundred years between 1870 and 1970—was primarily based in the industrial working class (though of course additional support, especially for the non-socialist left, came from reformist elements of the white-collar middle class and the agrarian sector). This coalition led by the industrial working class ebbed and flowed in this period but reached its peak of power and influence in the 30 years after World War II, resulting in the progressive welfare state that dominated the Western world. But this dominance did not last and one of the key reasons is very simple: the industrial working class had typically peaked in size by 1970 (in some countries somewhat earlier) and after 1970 experienced a precipitous decline. The general pattern has been a decline from 40 to 50 percent of the workforce to only around a quarter in a very short historical time span.

For example, in Germany the proportion of blue-collar workers (production, craft, operatives, transport, and manual labor) in the workforce has been cut in half since the late 1950s to just over one-quarter of the workforce today, while the proportion of white-collar workers has nearly tripled to 57 percent.[1] Similarly, in Sweden the proportion of blue-collar workers has been cut in half to one quarter of the workforce just since the mid-1970s.[2]

Closely related to this trend, employment in the industrial sector (mining, manufacturing, construction, utilities and transport) has dropped rapidly across countries, replaced by employment in the service sector. In Germany, the industrial sector has declined from 55 percent of employment in 1950 to just 26 percent today.[3] Similarly, in the Netherlands industrial employment dropped from 40 to 20 percent of the workforce between 1950 and 2003 and in the UK from 47 to 24 percent over the same period.[4]

In the United States, these changes have, if anything, been even stronger. The blue-collar workforce is now down to just 21 percent of workers and industrial employment is down to just 16 percent.[5]

To put these changes in perspective, consider that industrial employment in the United States, after rising for around 150 years, is now roughly back to the level it was in

1820, when 70 percent of employment was agricultural.[6] And now services are well over three-quarters of employment, so agriculture and services have essentially swapped places since 1820, while industry over this nearly 200-year time span has wound up back in the same place as a share of employment.

The profound significance of this remarkable change has yet to be fully absorbed by the left. Surely it is of earth-shaking significance that the class upon which progressive coalitions were built for so long has subsided back to its level of the early 1800s.

And there are related changes that deepen the significance of this shift in the class structure. For example, union membership, a traditional driver of left voting, has been steadily dropping across countries, as well as shifting its composition toward public sector employees. In the United States, union membership peaked at 35 percent of the non-agricultural workforce in the mid-1950s and is now down to about 11 percent and even lower (7 percent) in the private sector.[7]

Similarly, in the Netherlands, union membership has dropped from 37 to 21 percent of the workforce between 1979 and 2007. In Germany over the same period, unionization dropped from 35 to 20 percent. In the UK, the decline was from 52 to 29 percent; in Spain, from 43 to 15 percent.[8] Only the Nordic countries have been able to maintain their high union membership rates at close to their historic levels.

But even more significant is the glaring fact that, as the industrial working class has declined in numbers, it has become less supportive of traditional left parties. In Sweden, the social democrats' share of the LO (blue-collar workers union) vote has declined by 20 points from 1982 to 2010. In Denmark, social democrats' share of the traditional working-class vote declined by 17 points from the 1960s to the 1990s; in the UK by 18 points from the 1960s to the 2000s; and in France (in the second round of the presidential elections) by 19 points from 1974 to 2007.[9] And in the United States, the white sector of the working class is now more likely to vote Republican than Democratic in most elections.

Outside of the United States, there is also considerable variation in where the lost support from blue-collar workers is going. Some of it is going to the traditional right but in countries with strong multi-party systems much of that lost support has been finding its way to parties of the populist right (e.g., the Freedom Party in the Netherlands, the National Front in France, the Sweden Democrats in Sweden, the Danish People's Party in Denmark, JOBBIK in Hungary). A much smaller portion has typically migrated to parties of the populist left (e.g., the Socialist Party in Netherlands, the Left Party in Germany, the Socialist People's Party in Denmark). However, the recent emergence of new left populist parties like Podemos in Spain and Syriza in Greece indicates that the situation may be more fluid in Southern Europe.

In short, the old progressive coalition is dead; by dint of declining numbers and attenuating support, the industrial working class can no longer play a leading role in the broad left. The ongoing (indeed, never-ending) struggle to reform capitalism will have to be waged on a new basis.

The left in the United States is probably the farthest along in absorbing the implications of this change and building a new progressive coalition. Partially this reflects the fact that modernizing structural change is somewhat farther along in the United States, creating new left constituencies at a particularly rapid rate. But it also reflects the advantage the United States left gains from the simple two-party nature of the U.S. political system—the Democratic party is the natural, indeed only viable, vehicle for progressive constituencies, new and old. By contrast, in Europe, to a greater or lesser degree, the multi-party nature of political systems has brought to the fore a variety of left socialist, ecological (green) and social liberal parties to compete with social democrats, the traditional parties of the industrial working class. To make things even more complicated, these alternative left parties typically do disproportionately well among new constituencies, a development social democrats have had a hard time accepting. This has made it even harder in these countries to fully harness the political power of emerging constituencies.

These emerging constituencies reflect the broad structural shift away from manufacturing and toward a postindustrial, knowledge-based society embedded in a global economy. Accompanying this shift have been changes in family and values norms—lowered fertility, diversity in family forms, rise of postmaterial values, decline of traditional religion—sometimes referred to as the Second Demographic Transition.[10] Together these changes have given rise to an explosion of left-leaning groups that is making up for the decline of the traditional working class and powering the emergence of new left coalitions across the advanced Western world. Conservatives, in contrast, are relying ever more heavily on declining social sectors—very much including the traditional working class—to buoy their electoral fortunes.

RISING EDUCATIONAL LEVELS AND WHITE COLLARIZATION

The flip side of the decline in the traditional working class is the rise of white-collar and professional workers. As mentioned earlier, the proportion of white-collar workers (those in professional, managerial, technical and clerical-sales positions) in Germany's workforce has nearly tripled since the 1950s to almost 60 percent, and the rate of white collarization is not far off in other countries.[11] In the United States, the latest data have this group at around 61 percent with another 18 percent in the somewhat ambiguous service occupation category (which includes everything from medical assistants and police to janitors and waiters).[12] The rise of the white-collar workforce is a universal trend.

We can get a better sense of these shifts in the job structure by looking at data that reorganize and combine information on industry and occupation to better sort workers by skill levels and content of work performed. In *The Economy Goes to College* by economists Anthony Carnevale and Stephen Rose, workers are sorted into three occupation tiers: managerial/professional, middle-skill, and low-skill.[13] In this categorization, mid-skill jobs include not only supervisors, skilled crafts and clericals but also service occupations like medical assistants and police, while the low-skill category includes not just factory operatives but also retail sales clerks and service workers like security guards, janitors and waitresses. Today, 35 percent of jobs are managerial/professional, 36 percent are middle skill and just 29 percent are low skill. Managerial/professional positions are up 14 points as a share of jobs since 1967, with that increase mostly balanced by a decline of 10 points in the low-skill share of jobs.

Carnevale and Rose also combine data on occupation and industry to classify all workers by the content of the work they perform in the economy. This functional analysis produces a division of the workforce into five basic categories: office work (across all industries), high-skill services (non-office work in health care, education and communications), low-skill services (retail, personal and food services), manual labor in industry and primary production (mining, farming, fishing). Their analysis indicates that 44 percent of U.S. jobs today are in offices, with another 20 percent in high-skill services. Just 15 percent of jobs are manual labor in industry, with another 19 percent in low-skill services. Since 1967, the big change has been the rise in office work and high-skill services (up 14 points as a share of jobs), while the big decline has been in industrial manual labor, down 13 points. Interestingly, the share of low-skill service jobs is just about the same today as it was back in 1967.

Closely related to the "white collarization" of the economy is another universal trend: the rise in educational levels. Across Western advanced countries there has been a sharp decline in the ranks of those with the lowest levels of education and a rapid increase in those with the highest levels of education—college and advanced degrees. For example, in the Netherlands, the proportion at this educational level rose 15 points between 1985 and 2009[14] and in France this proportion rose 14 points between 1982 and 2006.[15]

The United States provides a particularly compelling example of rapidly rising educational levels. Incredible as it may seem today, in 1940 three-quarters of American adults 25 and over were high school dropouts (or never made it as far as high school), and just 5 percent had a four-year college degree or higher. But educational credentials exploded in the postwar period. By 1960, the proportion of adults lacking a high school diploma was down to 59 percent; by 1980, it was less than a third, and by 2014, it was down to only 12 percent. Concomitantly, the proportion with a BA or higher rose steadily and reached 32 percent in 2014. Moreover, those with some college (but not a four-year degree) constituted another 27 percent of the population, making a total of 59 percent—almost three in five—who had at least some college education.[16] Quite a change: moving from a country where the typical adult did not graduate high school (or even *reach* high school) to a country where the typical adult not only has a high school diploma but some college as well. This change, combined with the fact that nearly two-thirds of jobs are now in offices and high-skill services, gives a vivid sense of the scale of the transformation undergone by Western society.

These massive shifts represent a fundamental change in the terrain confronting today's left. The numbers are not there to build a progressive coalition based on manual labor, even if supplemented by low-skill service workers (which, keep in mind, are not a growing share of workers). Educated workers in offices and high-skill services have now become necessary building blocks of a new coalition.

Fortunately for the left, as postindustrial society has evolved, the highly educated have moved to the left, bolstering progressive coalitions across the Western world. In the United States, for example, in the aftermath of the Reagan revolution, Democrats did no better among white college-educated voters than they did among white non-college-educated (working-class) voters, who had moved sharply to the right. But that has changed significantly since then and now Democrats' margins are at least 12 points better among white college graduates than among white working-class voters.[17]

The most progressive element of the burgeoning white-collar population is professionals, who have the highest education levels. This group typically has forthrightly liberal views on social issues as well as moderately progressive tendencies on economic issues and a distaste for aggressive militarism in foreign policy.

Fifty years ago professionals were actually the most conservative occupational group in the United States. But over time—especially the last several decades—they have shifted to a strongly progressive stance. Professionals supported the Democratic candidate by an average of 52 percent to 40 percent in the 1988 to 2000 presidential elections. And in 2004 they moved still farther in this direction, supporting Kerry over Bush by a 63 percent to 37 percent margin.[18] Their support for Democrats has remained high ever since.[19]

Since professionals are a rapidly rising group in America and other Western countries, this pattern of support is highly beneficial to the left. In the 1950s professionals made up only about 7 percent of the workforce in the United States. But as the country has moved away from a blue-collar industrial economy to a postindustrial one that produces more ideas and services, that number has grown dramatically. Today they are 21 percent, triple their level in the 1950s.[20]

In Western Europe, the growth of the highly educated has kept pace with that in the United States and in some countries exceeded it. And as in the United States, that is broadly good for the left since the highly educated tend to lean progressive, especially professionals.[21] For example, in Germany in the 2013 federal election, college-educated voters voted for left parties (defined here and in other countries as all social democratic, green and left socialist/populist parties) at a rate 6 points higher than voters overall, and professionals did the same at a rate 9 points higher. Similarly, in the 2013 Austrian federal election, college-educated voters backed the left at a rate 15 points higher than all voters, and professionals supported the left at a rate 10 points higher. And in France, in the first round of presidential voting in 2012, college-educated voters voted left at a rate 9 points higher than all voters, and professionals likewise voted left at a rate 8 points higher.[22]

However, there is a wrinkle to this support that presents a challenge to the European left. Social democratic parties have been the mainstays of the left in Europe for a very long time, but have not necessarily received strong support from left-leaning professionals and highly educated voters. Instead, these groups tend to allocate an unusually high proportion of their left votes to green and left socialist/populist parties. As a result, professionals and the college-educated tend to vote at a lower rate for social democrats than voters as a whole, but at a much higher rate for the other segments of the left, particularly greens. For example, in the 2013 Austrian election, the non–social democratic left did 25 points better among the college-educated than among all voters and 18 points better among professionals; and in the 2013 German election, the corresponding figures were 15 and 14 points.[23]

Indeed, so strong has support become for greens and left populists among professionals and the highly educated that the combined votes for these parties frequently matches or exceeds support for the social democrats among these constituencies. This was true in the four countries mentioned above, as well as in Portugal, Spain and the Netherlands.[24]

It is also worth noting that professionals and the highly educated give disproportionately high support to centrist[25] parties.[26] This creates additional coalitional possibilities for the left, further disadvantaging the right.

IMMIGRANTS AND MINORITIES

Over the last few decades, the immigrant and minority population has increased substantially across countries and in most of them is continuing to increase. The United States is of course the poster child for this kind of change, since the minority population is both exceptionally large and exceptionally correlated with left voting (in 2008 and 2012 minorities voted 80 percent for the Democratic presidential candidate; in 2016, the analogous figure was 74 percent). In 1980, the population of the United States was 80 percent white. Today, that proportion has fallen to 63 percent and by the year 2060 it is projected to be under 44 percent. Hispanics were 6 percent in 1980, are 17 percent today and should be 29 percent by 2060. Asians/others were just

2 percent in 1980, are 8 percent today and should be 15 percent by 2060.[27]

Nothing captures the magnitude of these shifts better than the rise of majority-minority states.[28] Right now, there are only four of these states: California, Hawaii, New Mexico and Texas. But the next two majority-minority states, Maryland and Nevada, should arrive in the next five years. After that, there should be four more in the 2020s: Arizona, Florida, Georgia and New Jersey. In the 2030s, these states should be joined by Alaska, Louisiana and New York and in the 2040s by Connecticut, Delaware, Illinois, Mississippi, Oklahoma and Virginia. The 2050s should round out the list by adding Colorado, North Carolina and Washington state. That should bring the number of majority-minority states to 22, including 7 of the 10 currently largest states and 11 of the top 15. These states account for two-thirds of the nation's population.

Many other states are projected to be more than 40 percent minority by 2060, including Utah, Kansas, South Carolina, Pennsylvania, Michigan and Oregon. Even states such as Ohio, Indiana, Minnesota, Wisconsin, Nebraska, North Dakota, South Dakota, Wyoming and Montana should be well above 30 percent minority by that year.

Children will be the vanguard of diversity's spread as ever-more diverse generations are born and raised in every part of the United States. Arizona's children are already majority-minority at 60 percent; by 2060, they should be an astonishing 81 percent minority. By the same year, Florida's children could be 76 percent minority, and Connecticut's children could be 69 percent minority. Virginia's could be 63 percent minority, while Kansas's could be at 61 percent. Indeed, only six states in the country are projected to have less than 40 percent minority children by 2060.

Rising diversity is even affecting the oldest age group in the U.S. population, those 65 and over, who are projected to grow substantially as a share of eligible voters. In 1980, the 65+ age group was only 11 percent minority. Today, they are 22 percent minority. By 2060, minorities are projected to be close to half—45 percent—of this age group. Indeed, almost all the growth in the over-65 population in the future will be due to minorities, not whites.

Change is slower in Europe, but it is happening nonetheless. In the UK, the nonwhite (black, Asian and minority ethnic, or BAME) population is projected to reach 20 percent of the population by 2031, compared to 13 percent in 2001. In the Netherlands, the migrant population share is projected to reach 26 percent by 2040. In Spain, the immigrant population has grown from 200,000 to just under six million since 1981. In France, around 150,000 newly naturalized citizens are being added to the election rolls every year, which means 750,000 newly naturalized citizens participated as first-time voters in the 2012 presidential elections.[29]

Across European countries, as in the United States, the general tendency is for immigrant/minority voters to vote left. There are differences, however, by country of origin.

In Germany, for example, migrants from Turkey are particularly likely to vote left while migrants from the former Soviet Union are least likely to do so. In France, migrants of African origin (and their children) are most supportive of the left. In the UK, those of Caribbean origin are most supportive of the left, though all BAME subgroups display much higher left support rates than the rest of the population.[30]

In addition, immigrant/minority voters, in contrast to professionals and the highly educated, tend to give disproportionately high support to mainstream social democratic parties. But regardless of variation, the overall tendency is clear and unambiguous.[31] The rising immigrant/minority population is a boost for the left across advanced Western countries.

WOMEN

Historically, left parties have gotten more support from men than women. In recent elections, and across countries, this tendency has been reversed so that left parties tend to get more support from women than men. However, in most European countries this difference is more modest than in the United States, and has also arrived far later than in the United States, where women started voting more left than men back in the 1970s. But the uniformity of this trend is striking, confirming that women voters across countries have become increasingly important to progressive electoral success.

The key reason for the progressive trend among women is that the composition of the female population has changed in important ways, liberating women from their traditional constraints. Most obvious is the entry of women into the labor force and out of a home-bound role that tended to foster conservatism. It is also true that women have moved rapidly into the ranks of higher education and the professions, with their rate of advance frequently eclipsing that of men. And women are also much more likely to be single or to remain single than they were in the past.

This is why the left is strongest among the three subgroups of women who capture this pattern of change: those who are unmarried, those who are working and those who are highly educated. This pattern is strongest in the United States. Single women went for Obama by 70 percent to 29 percent in 2008 and by 67 percent to 31 percent in 2012; in 2016, single women supported Hillary Clinton over Donald Trump 63 percent to 32 percent. Women with a postgraduate education voted for Obama by 61 percent to 37 percent in 2012 and working women did the same by 56 percent to 41 percent.[32]

The number of women relative to the number of men is changing little, of course. But demographic trends within the female population have favored the left and should continue to do so. Unmarried women are now 49 percent, or almost half, of all adult women, up from 32 percent in 1974.[33] They currently make up more than a quarter of eligible voters—nearly the size of white evangelical Protestants, who are perhaps the GOP's largest base group. And since the current growth rate of the unmarried women population is relatively high, the proportion of unmarried women in the voting pool should continue to increase.

What's more, there is every expectation that this burgeoning population of unmarried women will continue to lean strongly left in their politics. Survey data consistently show this group to be unusually populist on economic issues and generally opposed to conservative foreign policy and social issue positions.[34]

DECLINE OF TRADITIONAL FAMILY
AND TRADITIONAL RELIGION

Across countries, the traditional family is declining and we are seeing a lot more single-person households. In the United States, unmarried adults have risen from 30 to 47 percent of all adults between 1974 and 2014 and have risen from 23 to 41 percent of all voters between 1974 and 2012.[35] In the UK, the number of single-person households rose by 73 percent between 1981 and 2008. And in the Netherlands, the proportion of unmarried voters in the 20–65 age group increased from 26 to 36 percent in just 12 years (1998–2010).[36]

By and large, this burgeoning population of unmarried voters is more likely to support the left than their married counterparts across advanced countries. As noted above, this is a very strong tendency among unmarried women but it is also quite strong among unmarried men. For example, in 2012 unmarried men supported Obama by 56–40, not as strong to be sure as the 67–31 margin among unmarried women, but solid support nonetheless.[37] Overall, it seems clear that the ongoing trend toward more single-person households is of benefit to progressives.

Along with the traditional family, traditional religion is declining and secularism is on the rise. In the Netherlands, the number of those with no religion almost doubled, from 23 percent of the population to 44 percent, between 1971 and 2009. Similarly, in France, those with no religion rose from 13 to 30 percent between 1988 and 2007.[38] And, despite the tendency of recent immigrants to be more religious than average, the most rapidly increasing religious group in the United States is those without any religious affiliation, who rose from 16 to 23 percent of adults in just seven years (2007–2014).[39]

Other changes to the traditional religious universe include increases in those with non-Christian religious faiths and a general decline in religious observance among those who retain a Christian faith.

On one level, these changes indirectly benefit the left since they undercut traditional linkages between religion and politics, which have typically benefited conservative parties. More directly, secular, less-observant and non-Christian voters tend to lean left politically. In the 2012 presidential election in the United States, Obama carried 70 percent of those with no religion, 69 percent of

Jews, 74 percent of those with other non-Christian religions and 62 percent of the unobservant.[40] In the 2016 election, Clinton's support among these groups was close to Obama's: 67 percent, 71 percent, 62 percent and 62 percent, respectively.

This pattern is also strong in advanced European countries. For example, in both the German and Austrian 2013 federal elections, those who do not attend religious services except on special occasions voted for left parties at a rate 8 points higher than voters overall. And in France, in the 2012 election, non-attenders voted left at a 7 points higher rate than all voters; in the 2011 Spanish election, the corresponding figure was 14 points.[41]

Complicating this tendency is the same wrinkle in left support noted for professionals and the highly educated. Non-attenders also tend to allocate an unusually high proportion of their left votes to green and left socialist/populist parties. In the 2013 Austrian election and in the 2011 Spanish election, the non–social democratic left did 12 points better among non-attenders than among all voters; in the 2011 Finnish election and in the 2011 Danish election, the corresponding figure was 10 points.[42]

THE RISE OF THE MILLENNIAL GENERATION

Into this brave new postindustrial world steps the Millennial generation (defined here as those born between 1981 and 2000). As of 2016, they compose all of the 18–35 voters and will continue to do so for another couple of years, after which a new generation will start entering the electorate. In this generation, all the trends summarized in this chapter find their strongest expression. Compared to previous generations at the same age, Millennials are less likely to be working class, more likely to be highly educated, more likely to be professionals (or in training to be), more likely to be of a minority or migrant background, more likely to be single and more likely to be secular in religious orientation. They are in short the vessels of postindustrial modernity, with an outlook—particularly among women—that is notably cosmopolitan, tolerant and open compared to previous generations.

It is difficult to overstate the significance of this particular demographic shift. The one true inevitability in demographic change is the replacement of older generations by newer generations. The Millennial generation and its attitudes therefore provide a glimpse of the political future across advanced countries.

In 1980, the eligible U.S. electorate still contained a large contingent—32 percent—from the Greatest and Lost (born before 1928) generations, along with 28 percent from the Silent generation and a dominant 41 percent from the Baby Boom generation. Today, it is a different world: The Greatest generation has all but vanished, and the Silent generation, the most conservative generation in the current electorate, is down to 11 percent of eligibles. The Baby Boomers are still a substantial presence at 31 percent of eligibles, though down substantially from their peak of 45 percent in 1982. But the newer generations now dominate the electorate: Generation X at 26 percent of eligible voters and the Millennial generation at 31 percent, matching the Boomers, form the majority. And by 2030, the Millennial generation alone, plus its successor generation, the post-Millennials, will constitute the majority of eligibles.[43] Moreover, the Millennial generation, whose turnout rates are currently relatively low, is certain to vote in larger numbers as its members age, further enhancing this generation's political influence.

In Europe, the impact of generational replacement tends be to be felt more slowly because of the smaller relative size of the Millennial generation compared to earlier generations in most of these countries. However, the same general patterns of replacement apply and will transform the European electorate over time.

As we would expect from the attitudes and characteristics of Millennials, this generation leans left in most countries. In the United States, Millennials are by far the most left-leaning generation, voting for and identifying with the Democrats at a rate far higher than older generations.[44] In the 2008 presidential election, 18- to 29-year-old Millennials voted 66 percent Democratic; in 2012 they voted 60 percent Democratic; and in 2016 they voted 55 percent Democratic.[45]

Similar tendencies can be seen in advanced European countries but with a familiar twist. As noted earlier, emerging demographic groups in these countries tend to lean left, but also to look past traditional left parties to a wide array of green and left socialist/populist parties. This tendency is particularly marked for the younger generation.

For example, in the 2011 Finnish election, Millennial generation voters supported the non–social democratic left at a rate 20 points higher than the overall electorate; in the 2014 Swedish election the corresponding figure was 14 points; and in the 2013 Austrian and 2015 Portuguese elections, the advantage was 9 points. Indeed, as seen earlier for professionals and the college educated, Millennial voters' combined support for green and left populist parties has frequently matched or exceeded their support for traditional social democratic parties in European countries. And, as we also saw earlier for these educated groups, Millennial voters have generally showed disproportionate support for centrist parties, further disadvantaging the right and creating coalitional possibilities for the left.[46]

IF YOU'RE SO (DEMOGRAPHICALLY) SMART,
WHY AREN'T YOU RICH?

The trends just outlined will continue in the future. The chances they will reverse themselves are nil. It is open to debate how fast these changes will be in the future; that these changes will take place is not.

If that is true, why is the left not doing better than it is? Why is the right doing such a good job holding back progressive advance, despite the demographic wind at progressives' back?

Some reasons for this are structural. In the United States, a combination of geographical concentration of Democratic constituencies and outright gerrymandering gives the left a disadvantage in competing for seats in the House of Representatives, while the small-state bias in the Senate (Wyoming gets the same number of senators as California) similarly disadvantages the left in the upper chamber.

In Europe, the nature of electoral systems has enabled the diffusion of the left vote across multiple parties, making it harder to coordinate emerging progressive strength. This makes it more difficult to maximize the left vote, as well as to turn even a majority into actual governance. As one example among many, in 2013 the German left (Social Democrats, Greens, Left Party) obtained a majority of seats but the Social Democrats ruled out working with the Left Party and turned instead to a "grand coalition" with the Christian Democrats, the main party of the right.

These structural factors are important and they undeniably hold back the left. But they are not the main problem. The main problem is that the new progressive coalition itself has been difficult to keep mobilized and has not been strong enough to fend off the backlash-driven strategies of the right. This reflects the simple fact that the left has been unable to give these emerging constituencies what they want.

Consider that the unifying thread running through progressives' emerging constituencies is their aspirational nature. They either tend to be labor market outsiders who aspire to become insiders (minorities, Millennials, women, especially single and working women) or holders of relatively large amounts of human capital (professionals and the highly educated) who aspire to high economic mobility and a high quality of life. This necessitates a strong role for government, but one that shifts progressive policy priorities from *security* to *opportunity*. The latter entails an emphasis on the acquisition and use of education; the development of new economic sectors that can provide high-skill, high-wage jobs; investment in infrastructure that can support rising economic sectors and the transition to a green economy; the provision of public amenities; and the achievement and maintenance of full employment.

This does not mean jettisoning economic security programs. But it does mean a shift of emphasis so that these programs do not interfere with mobility and, in fact, serve it. Without a basic level of economic security, survival and the avoidance of economic catastrophe rule workers' lives and limit energy for economic improvement. At this level, economic security is both humane and good for mobility. Too much economic security, however, especially if concentrated on labor market insiders through rigid labor market protections and benefits, prevents full employment and drains money from the public sector that could be used for opportunity-enhancing investment in education and infrastructure. That's bad for mobility.

So progressives will need to change their current priorities to serve their emerging coalition. This will alienate some supporters in the traditional working class—we have already seen this—but it will also serve to attract and retain the aspirational members of this group, as well as cementing the support of emerging constituencies. Not only is this a tradeoff worth making, but it is realistically the only way forward for the left.

On one level, this might seem like an easy choice. There are few priorities more popular than enhancing opportunity. The idea that we should do everything possible to ensure everyone has an equal opportunity to succeed generates around 90 percent support or higher in multiple polls. Lack of opportunity is typically viewed as the biggest barrier to economic success; conversely, providing the opportunity for everyone to succeed is generally viewed as more important than redistribution alone by margins of 2:1 or 3:1. Indeed, careful reviews of public opinion data on inequality and opportunity indicate that Americans' chief objection to greater economic inequality is that it makes it more difficult for the average citizen to move up the economic ladder.[47] That is, what Americans object to most vigorously about economic inequality is not that it causes suffering—though they do object to that—but that it restricts economic mobility.

So what is standing in the left's way?

One problem is that recognition of the shape and composition of the emerging progressive coalition has been slow and was linked initially to a political program known as "The Third Way." The Third Way posited that the structure of capitalist societies was indeed changing and that the traditional working class was becoming less important. But the analysis went little beyond observations on the white collarization of work and the assertion that the left was best served by leaving capitalism alone to generate riches that could be redistributed and repurposed.[48] The former view showed only a crude understanding of the depth of the social transformation affecting Western industrial societies, while the latter was simply wrong as an assessment of contemporary capitalism's ability to function well without proper guidance and regulation.

This brings us to the nub of the matter. Without relatively fast and equally distributed economic growth, it will be very difficult, if not impossible, to provide adequate levels of economic mobility for progressives' emerging coalition, the key to consolidating progressive strength. Third Way advocates thought they had found the right approach to producing such growth. They had not.

But perhaps they deserve points for trying. It is certainly no worse, and perhaps better, than accepting the current slow growth/unequal distribution environment as unchangeable and concentrating the left's energies on defending existing welfare state programs within that environment. That is predictably ineffective as a left strategy, as the European social democrats, in particular, have found out. Indeed, European social democrats have seen their support crater again and again to historic lows, whether they were working outside government as the "responsible" opposition, or inside government, attempting to make economic austerity slightly less toxic (frequently in grand coalitions with the center-right).

These developments provide yet more support for the good times theory of left advance. Lacking such good times, the left will continue to flounder.

So how do we get to such good times? The experience of advanced Western countries in the last 40 years, and particularly since the Great Financial Crisis, indicates these good times will not be forthcoming until capitalism's "Piketty problem" is directly addressed by the left. What capitalism's Piketty problem is and why and how the left will be forced to address it is the subject of the next chapter.

THREE

From Capitalism's Piketty Problem to the Opportunity State

WHAT MARX GOT WRONG (AND RIGHT)

Capitalism has always had its critics. The most famous and perhaps the most vociferous was Karl Marx. Marx argued that the basic economic dynamic of capitalism leads to the immiseration of workers and, eventually, to systemic crisis and the failure of growth, as the rate of profit falls and capital becomes concentrated in fewer and fewer hands. Only socialism could correct this situation.

Marx was certainly on to something in linking the underlying logic and tendencies of capitalism to serious economic and social problems. However, in most of his specific claims he was wrong and very much a prisoner of the times in which he wrote. Most notably, the immiseration of the working class did not last and worsen as he thought it would, based on his observations of the early stages of the Industrial Revolution in England. Ironically, by the time he published his first volume of *Capital* in 1867, these early stages were over and real wages and living standards in England and other capitalist countries were rising and would continue to do so,[1] albeit at considerably varying rates, to our present day. Marx simply did not anticipate how technological improvements and ongoing, durable rises in productivity could translate into elevated living standards for workers, nor, of course, did he foresee how government intervention and welfare state measures could help sand off capitalism's rough edges and channel more benefits to workers. In this sense, Marx's theory did a good job of predicting the past but was too tied to that past to be much of a useful guide to the future of workers under capitalism.

Not only did the immiseration of the proletariat fail to continue, but his predictions of systemic collapse also failed to come true. The rate of profit did not continue to fall, leading to anarchic inter-capitalist competition and squeezed workers in mass revolt. The capitalist system certainly lurched and faltered at times but fell well short of the apocalyptic ending Marx anticipated.

These realities, combined with the demonstrable failure

of self-described "socialist" countries to match the economic performance of capitalist countries, led to a steady revision of most of Marx's claims by those who identified with his thought and outright rejection of these claims by most on the broad left. Indeed, the remarkable economic progress after World War II, where working-class living standards soared across advanced countries, led to general acceptance on the left of the Keynesian welfare state as essentially a new and fairer stage of capitalism.

The view that this was the natural order of things received reinforcement from the views of leading economic theorists like Simon Kuznets, who posited a U-shaped curve of development for capitalist societies.[2] The basic idea was that societies at a low stage of development were quite equal and then rapidly became very unequal as development proceeded and the early stages of the Industrial Revolution kicked in (the stage that Marx necessarily focused on). But as the Industrial Revolution consolidated itself and productivity growth took off, democratic capitalist societies naturally evolved toward a more equal distribution of the benefits of growth. When Kuznets was writing in the 1950s this seemed to make a great deal of sense. But, like Marx, his theory was great at predicting the past, but less useful in divining the future.

As it turned out, and as was touched on in the previous chapter, the natural evolution of capitalism began to seem less benign and more problematic starting in the 1970s when growth slowed, unemployment rose, inequality started to widen, and the Keynesian welfare state proved far less robust than the left had assumed. This led to the counter-attack by conservative economics, which successfully cast the welfare state as a shackle on capitalist advance and an enemy of rising living standards. The only way out, conservatives argued, was to unleash the natural dynamic of capitalism, which, left to its own unregulated devices, would produce the best economic outcomes. "There Is No Alternative" (frequently abbreviated to TINA), British conservative leader Margaret Thatcher famously proclaimed. The left, struggling to defend the gains embodied in the welfare state, but no longer confident in their own economic model, wound up agreeing that government should mostly get out of the way of a finance-heavy, globalizing capitalism but still strive to provide welfare state benefits in a lean, fiscally responsible, economically efficient way.

This benign and hands-off view of capitalism, with the de-Keynesianized welfare state as a kind of poor relation, came to be known as the Third Way and dominated left thinking across advanced countries in the 1990s and early 2000s.[3] As the latter decade unfolded, however, with stagnating living standards and worsening inequality, resistance to the free pass given to capitalism stiffened on the left. And that was before the Great Financial Crisis of 2008–09 arrived and laid low the economies of all advanced nations. A crisis of this magnitude wasn't supposed to happen, not just according to conservative economists, but according to the many left economists who had bought into the rosier, Third Way–style view of capitalism.

THE GREAT FINANCIAL CRISIS AND CAPITALISM'S "PIKETTY PROBLEM"

The very slow recovery from this huge crash, exacerbated by bouts of austerity medicine, particularly in Europe, has produced years of economic pain and insecurity for broad swaths of the population.[4] In the United States, where recovery has generally been stronger than in Europe, median household income was still $3,000 less in 2014 than its pre-crash peak in 1999—15 years before.[5] And it has not gone unnoticed that recovery across countries has gone a great deal quicker for the wealthy than for the middle class and the poor, intensifying already-existing inequality. Contrary to the benign view that capitalism produces good outcomes with minimal nudging, the developments of the last 40 years—especially the last 10—suggest that capitalism may have innate, systemic tendencies toward highly unequal, and occasionally catastrophic, outcomes.

Call it capitalism's "Piketty problem," after French economist Thomas Piketty's magisterial work, *Capital in the Twenty-First Century*.[6] Piketty's work made a huge splash after it appeared in English translation in 2014 both because of its exceptional—indeed unprecedented—empirical documentation and because it spoke clearly and rigorously to people's sense that modern economies have fundamental, not episodic, problems.

The essence of Piketty's argument is that capitalism, left to itself, does not produce ever-more equal outcomes, but, *contra* Kuznets, naturally tends toward high levels of inequality, toward divergence rather than convergence. This does not mean there are no forces for convergence. The diffusion of knowledge and skills over time is a very powerful force in this direction, as common sense and economic analysis suggest.

However, the forces for divergence can be more powerful still, as we have been seeing in the last 40 years, and, Piketty argues, as we are likely to see in the rest of the twenty-first century. This is where Piketty really strikes a nerve. It is one thing to clearly describe how income and wealth inequality are growing in advanced societies and provide a convincing analysis of same. It is quite another for that analysis to provide a solid theoretical and empirical case that people's greatest fears about the current age of inequality are completely justified: as bad as things are, they are highly likely to get worse—indeed, much worse.

This will be the result, Piketty argues, if economic growth rates continue to be modest, ensuring, in his famous equation, that $r > g$, where r is the rate of return on capital and g is the growth rate. This inequality leads inexorably to a rise in the ratio of capital to income in the economy and the increasing concentration of wealth at the top of the social structure.

Reinforcing this trend is the increasing inequality of income itself. It is not the case, as standard economic theory would have it, that inequality of income under capitalism is simply a natural reflection of differences in productivity. Compensation in modern economies, particularly in the United States, can diverge and has diverged radically from this ideal, as norms and policy regimes that held inequality in check have disintegrated. As a result, the highest earners—the "supermanagers" in Piketty's term—increasingly decide how to reward themselves and each other, with predictable results.[7]

Going forward, there appears to be little to stop these trends from continuing to drive inequality ever upward. Potentially, the trends toward wealth and income inequality could become so entwined that together they could produce "levels of inequality never before seen" in the twenty-first century.[8] This is a bleak picture but it accords very well with most people's sense of what has happened and where we are going on our current course.

And that's not all. Rising inequality clearly played an important role in the Great Financial Crisis of 2008–09, as the struggling bottom 90 percent took on more and more debt in the years preceding the crisis, aided and abetted by a burgeoning financial industry seeking investment outlets for wealthy clients with little regard for risk. Regulations on the financial industry have been tightened but if inequality is a root cause of instability then continuously rising inequality puts capitalist economies at great risk in the future.

Then there is the general problem of growth. It has become increasingly obvious from academic research and the experience of the last 40 years that highly unequal societies are not well-suited to fast growth. On the contrary, inequality past a level that provides reasonable rewards for entrepreneurship, skill acquisition and performance is actually a drag on growth, subtracting consumer demand from the economy, promoting destabilizing consumer debt, reducing human capital acquisition, breaking down social trust, stifling economic mobility and encouraging rent-seeking unproductive economic activity by the wealthy.

Therein lies the Piketty problem of contemporary capitalism:

1. The basic dynamic of the system tends toward higher inequality.

2. This reduces the effectiveness of economic growth in raising living standards.

3. Sluggish growth of living standards could potentially be mitigated by faster overall economic growth, even if it is unequally distributed.

4. But rising inequality slows down economic growth, rather than speeds it up, so that avenue is closed off as well.

Result: a vicious cycle of rising inequality, stagnating living standards and slowing economic growth.

That's the Piketty problem. And contemporary capitalism, left to its own devices, is highly unlikely to solve it.

CAN THE PIKETTY PROBLEM BE SOLVED?

So, is there a way out of this vicious cycle? Yes there is, once we accept the idea that capitalism cannot be expected to break out of it on its own. Instead, capitalism must be actively pointed in a different direction by adopting a new approach that pushes back against inequality and promotes the economic health of the middle and working classes as the key driver of growth. That is, instead of seeing the economic health of the great middle of society as simply a desirable outcome of growth, this new approach posits that a thriving middle is what allows the attainment of relatively fast growth. Conversely, high inequality is seen as not just unfair and injurious to those who come out on the short end of the stick but as an active obstacle to growth.[9]

Known generally as "equitable growth" or "middle-out" economics, this new approach is fast gaining adherents on the left. As currently articulated it has three broad components: (1) measures to directly improve economic outcomes for the working and middle classes; (2) measures to directly reduce the flow of excessive benefits to the wealthy; and (3) measures to increase societal investment in the jobs of the future.

Measures to directly improve economic outcomes generally include the following. First, there is the provision of more and more widely distributed educational opportunity. This provision is absolutely central to the life chances and economic mobility of the working and middle classes. Making early childhood education available for all is part of this, as is more effective elementary and secondary education and much easier access to a college education. Raising the quality and quantity of educational attainment helps individual workers but it does much more. As noted earlier, broad diffusion of knowledge and skills is a powerful countervailing force on rising inequality. And the role of rising societal skill levels in promoting economic growth is well documented.[10]

Policies to directly support wages are also important. A relatively high minimum wage, indexed to prices, fits in here, as do pro-work tax credits like the Earned Income Tax Credit and employee profit-sharing, share-ownership and representation. And, critically, the attainment and maintenance of full employment, including government as employer of last resort, will do a great deal to push wages up over the long term.[11]

Then there is the role of robust social insurance and social benefits.[12] Besides the familiar old-age programs of Social Security and Medicare, this includes the universal provision of health care, affordable child care, retirement savings accounts, paid sick and parental leave and paid vacation.

There is no question these measures would go a long way toward improving the lot of the working and middle classes in contemporary capitalism. But the equitable growth approach entails going beyond directly helping the great middle to cutting the flow of excessive benefits to the wealthy.

One part of this is increasing taxes on the wealthy and on wealth. As Piketty argues, low marginal income tax rates on the wealthy encourage the pursuit of extreme incomes, while much higher marginal rates can be implemented without adverse effects on work effort and entrepreneurship.[13] He also advocates for a modest tax on net wealth, ideally global in scope but at least on a regional basis. The political/institutional difficulties of such an arrangement are obvious but it should nevertheless be considered for its potential high utility.

Curtailing wealth through tax increases on the wealthy would, by definition, make a contribution toward reducing inequality by pushing down excess at the top of the income distribution. These measures would also have the highly desirable side effect of helping raise revenue for needed social programs and government investments to lift up the great middle of society (even if such taxes, by themselves, would not be sufficient to provide all the revenue needed).

There is also the issue of laws and incentives that encourage excessive and destabilizing wealth accumulation. A host of changes are needed here. Measures to combat these tendencies include ending "too big to fail" in the financial sector; enacting a financial transactions tax to discourage short-term, speculative investments; and eliminating tax loopholes on performance pay and other forms of compensation that have allowed CEO pay to skyrocket.

Direct measures to lift up the middle and push down the top are clearly necessary and important parts of an equitable growth program. But they are not sufficient. Sustained healthy economic growth also depends on increased long-term societal investment in the infrastructure, research and sectoral innovation that will underpin the jobs of the future.

There are obviously a lot of moving parts here. But several things are clear. There has been a systematic tendency to underinvest in infrastructure, both its maintenance and expansion, to suit the needs of modern postindustrial economies. This tendency has been particularly acute in the United States, where investment in infrastructure is now at historical lows, despite an immense backlog of deferred maintenance and mostly unfilled needs for new infrastructure.

This underinvestment reflects in large part unwarranted faith in the ability of the private sector to "go it alone" and drive growth purely on the basis of entrepreneurship and profit seeking. This ignores, of course, the well-known economic problem of "public goods" that are useful and necessary for many economic actors but are available to all—regardless of whether or not they have contributed anything to the availability of the public good ("free-riding")—and that cannot be appropriated for the exclusive use of any profit-making firm. Infrastructure is a classic example of such a public good, as is much basic scientific research that underpins existing industries (for example, NIH-funded health research).

In the absence of a robust supply of public goods, some firms will still make healthy profits and economic growth will still continue. But growth will be less than it otherwise would be and it will be tilted toward areas where large profits do not depend on public goods (think finance). Good for those firms that do make large profits, bad for the working and middle classes.

Worse, the problem goes beyond that indicated by the public goods framework. As economist Mariana Mazzucato points out, the role of the state is not just to supply needed public goods the private sector ignores (though this is very important) but also to be an entrepreneurial agent investing in areas that are far off the private sector's radar screen because of extreme uncertainty about economic returns.[14] This is particularly the case with fundamental knowledge generation and very early investments in new technological sectors. Current theories of economic growth assign such innovation a key role in economic growth and it is the "entrepreneurial state," in Mazzucato's phrase, which can afford—and is willing—to bear the inherently immeasurable risks of such innovation.

This has been the case in the United States, where pretty much all research underlying the internet and modern computing was funded and initially capitalized by the U.S. state. For example, the immensely profitable Apple corporation's signature products, like the iPhone and iPad, rest on fundamental innovations developed by government funding.[15] This includes everything from the internet to GPS to touch screens to Siri voice recognition. In other words, no entrepreneurial state, no Apple.

More generally, a Brookings Institution study found that 18 of the 25 most important breakthroughs in computer technology in the seminal 1946–65 period were underwritten by the federal government.[16] And it's not just information technology where the role of the state has been critical: between 1971 and 2006, 77 out of the 88 most important innovations *outside* of computing/communications,[17] as rated by *R&D Magazine*, were heavily dependent on government support, especially in their earliest developmental stages.

The role of the entrepreneurial state has been critical to growth in the past and there is no reason to think it will not be critical in the future. Progress in such emerging fields as biotechnology, nanotechnology and, of paramount importance, green technology will continue to depend on the entrepreneurial state being willing to provide support in areas where the private sector sees only unknowable risks. And without such progress, economic growth will fall well short of potential.

THE OPPORTUNITY STATE

Overall, it is the aim of the equitable growth vision of the state to improve both the quality and quantity of economic growth. In this, it can be distinguished from the post–World War II model of the classic welfare state, where emphasis was on post-market redistribution by the state and basic economic security. Call it the "opportunity state."

The prime directive of the opportunity state is to promote massive upward mobility for the working and middle classes by achieving the highest possible levels of economic growth and providing the great middle with the tools to grow along with the economy—to take advantage of opportunity. This includes a certain level of economic security, as embodied in wage floors, social insurance programs and mandated basic benefits. But security is not the end goal of such measures—rather, the goal is to provide opportunity to rise by taking away the endless struggle to simply exist day to day and avoid financial catastrophe.

In this sense, the opportunity state is antithetical to measures that encourage workers in protected sectors to stay in one place, make it difficult for entrepreneurs to start new businesses or allow workers to leave the labor market at very early ages. The purpose of economic security in the opportunity state is to make it universally easier for workers to move around, achieve upward mobility and prosper. Measures that divide the labor market into insiders, whose security is ironclad, and outsiders, who have none, are to be avoided. The goal is a labor market that is both flexible and underpinned by reasonable levels of economic security. This is the "flexicurity" model pioneered by the Nordic states of Europe, a good fit for the opportunity state going forward.

The opportunity state is thus the logical successor to the welfare state, an active state for the twenty-first century. But it is undeniably a robust vision of the state, which, while having a lighter and different hand in key areas, nevertheless envisions a large role for the state—indeed in some areas significantly larger than today. Could this happen or have we already reached the limit on how large the state can be?

Not if history is any guide. In all advanced societies, the state, as measured by spending as a share of GDP over time, has grown larger over time, albeit in an irregular rather than steady pattern. But the end result is clear. In the United States, for example, government spending was only 7 percent of GDP at the beginning of the twentieth century. Today, it is around 37 percent. Of course, the percentage is higher in most other industrialized countries, reaching around 60 percent in the prosperous Nordic countries of Denmark and Sweden. Indeed, the United States could add 10 percentage points to the GDP share of government spending—about enough to cover the programs enumerated above to lift up the working and middle classes—and still be only in the middle of the pack of today's advanced countries.[18]

Such a development might strike some as radically infeasible because Americans famously are not fond of big government and, depending on how survey questions are asked, declare their lack of interest in a general expansion of government's role. But such a view misunderstands the dominant ideology in America, which combines what political scientists Christopher Ellis and James Stimson refer to as "symbolic conservatism" (honoring tradition, distrusting novelty, embracing the conservative label) with "operational liberalism" (wanting government to do more and spend more in a wide variety of areas). In their definitive book, *Ideology in America*, they characterize symbolic conservatism as:

. . . fundamentally different from culturally conservative politics as defined by the religious right. It is respect for basic values: hard work, striving, caution, prudence, family, tradition, God, citizenship and the American flag. . . . [I]t is the mainstream culture. . . . It is woven into the fabric of how ordinary Americans live their lives.

And on operational liberalism they note:

Social Security is . . . no exception. Most Americans like most government programs. Most of the time, on average, we want government to do more and spend more. It is no accident we have created the programs of the welfare state. They were created—and are sustained—by massive public support.[19]

So there would appear to be no insuperable ideological obstacle to a substantially expanded role for government in a twenty-first-century opportunity state.[20] Indeed, such an expansion is fully in accord with Americans' durable commitment to operational liberalism.

Of course these expanded government programs, and other changes that are integral to the new opportunity state, will not happen all at once. Far from it. Like the programs of the past, they will be phased in gradually over time, in fits and starts, frequently in inefficient and suboptimal forms. That's the messy business of politics in a democracy. But happen they will and once enacted they will be hard to get rid of; instead, just as in the past, the programs will be modified, improved and even expanded. The reason is simple: people like programs that make their lives better and are far more likely to respond to program defects by demanding they be fixed than by demanding programs be eliminated.

Not only will the opportunity state be built in fits and starts, the left will adopt the opportunity state only in fits and starts as well. There are historical legacies and ingrained political habits to be overcome. But as the postindustrial progressive coalition continues to grow, the left will have no choice but to promote the opportunity state as the only vehicle capable of solving capitalism's Piketty problem and meeting the needs of its support base. The opportunity state, in short, will be the new TINA.

Naturally, limping along and letting current economic trends continue will be tempting because the challenge of change is real, but ultimately politicians on the left will take up the challenge because they want to generate reliable voting support and govern successfully (though it is inevitable, as we have seen, that they will try the easy ways first). This will be true of the Democratic Party in the United States and it will also be true of the more fragmented left in Europe, who apparently will have to be dragged kicking and screaming to cooperate with one another and turn back the conservatives.

THE LEFT'S MAGIC INGREDIENT: GROWTH

And of course, there is a magic ingredient for the left to make progress and build the opportunity state: growth. Solid, healthy growth will grease the wheels for left success; tepid growth and hard times will make everything more difficult. But how possible is such growth?

One line of argument about the economic future is that, while it might be possible to grow more equitably without hurting growth, prospects for faster growth are very limited. This is because advanced societies are already more or less at their growth frontier and the best one can hope for is modest tweaks to an underlying slow growth rate. If so, this would be problematic for the left, whose prospects are brighter when growth is relatively rapid.

But such a view is way too gloomy, for several reasons. One is that growth has been substantially higher in the past than it has been in recent decades and especially since the dawn of the new century.

Economic growth can be broken down into two

components: real GDP per capita growth and population growth. Of the two, it is more important to look at per capita GDP growth, since this is the growth that raises average living standards. Per capita economic growth in the United States between 1946 and 1973 was 2.4 percent a year, about doubling per capita GDP over those 26 years. In contrast, since 1973, the end of the postwar Keynesian era and the beginning of the Age of Inequality, per capita economic growth has been only 1.7 percent per year, again about doubling GDP per capita but over a far longer 46-year period. And since 2000, per capita growth has been particularly dismal: just 0.9 percent per year. The pattern is broadly similar in other advanced Western countries.[21]

Thus, as a number of observers have remarked,[22] we have received no growth dividend from the various policy and political choices that have led to our current levels of inequality. On the contrary, it seems more likely that these choices have left potential growth on the table, a pattern that is consistent with recent research on the relationship between rising inequality and the level and duration of economic growth. So the basic data suggest there is plenty of room for advanced capitalist economies to have higher growth rates.

That is, unless we believe there is something intrinsic to today's capitalist economies that dooms them to slow growth. But why would we believe that when there are so many plausible suspects in the policy realm to blame for recent slow growth rates?

AUSTERITY IN HISTORY AND TODAY

Start with the most basic policy problem we have today—the preference for budget austerity over Keynesian macroeconomic policies in many Western countries. It is striking how, in country after country, austerity was quickly adopted after the worst of the Great Financial Crisis was over, but way before economic growth had returned to pre-crisis levels. The result has been remarkably slow economic recoveries in most countries and continued high unemployment rates. This is policy error of the most elementary and egregious kind.

Where did this preference for austerity policies come from? The lineage of austerity goes back to the early liberal (in the European sense) economic thinkers, John Locke, David Hume and Adam Smith, all of whom played a role in theorizing and legitimizing market economics and all of whom tended to counterpose the virtues of market economics to the problem of predatory states (states that in those days were controlled by capricious sovereigns rather than elected representatives).[23] The state was, at best, a regrettable necessity whose powers of taxation and debt issuance made it highly likely that it would be a parasite on the economy and interfere with the market. Locke and Hume were particularly strong on this point, seeing little role for government beyond national defense and almost all government debt as bad. Smith had a somewhat more balanced view but in the end saw government's ability to accumulate and issue debt as inevitably eroding the private savings that lead to dynamic economic growth. Hence the need for a state that was as austere as possible.

Building on the work of David Ricardo and others in the nineteenth century, these anti-state and anti–public debt views eventually became codified into a system of economic thinking we know today as classical economics. This system provided a rigorous theoretical gloss to the emerging doctrine of austerity. According to classical economists, the overall economy tended toward a full employment equilibrium where all resources were productively employed. While this equilibrium could be temporarily disturbed by wage and price rigidities, misguided monetary policies and other things that distorted the market, the economy would quickly return to a full employment equilibrium once these distortions were eased. The role for government in responding to recession was therefore to do nothing, letting prices and wages fall to their natural levels or, even better, to actively cut spending, since government spending simply crowds out the private spending necessary to get the economy back into equilibrium. That is why, prior to Keynes, the orthodox budgetary approach to recessions was to cut, not increase, government spending so as to create the proper business environment and hasten the arrival of a new equilibrium.

Keynes didn't buy all this, seeing it as inconsistent with the behavior of real world economies, especially the ones he was observing at the time. In his view, the normal state of capitalist economies was not full employment, because total demand in the economy could easily fall short of total supply, creating equilibria with high levels of unemployment—the reverse of the classical precept that supply creates its own demand (Say's Law).

Keynes argued that because these equilibria were a natural and recurring tendency of capitalism, there was no natural adjustment process that would lead a market economy back to full employment. Nor could monetary policy—lowering interest rates or increasing the money supply—always be relied upon to jolt businesses back into action and increase employment. Instead, government must frequently step in to make up shortfalls in demand through fiscal policy—in other words, through government spending.

Keynes' anti-austerity ideas had their day, of course— and, as we have seen, a very successful day it was, lasting from the mid-1930s to the mid-1970s. But austerity ideas never went away because, as noted, they are rooted in an entire philosophy about the state and public debt that is not subject to disproof, especially among the conservative forces and big economic interests who embrace it. As a result, when Keynesian economics appeared to falter in the 1970s, austerity-based economics came roaring back and dominated economic thinking for the decades leading up to Great Financial Crisis and, after a brief resurgence of Keynesian economics in 2008–2010, came back yet again.[24] Austerity again dominates today's economic discussions (though less so in the United States than in other advanced Western countries), this time with the chimera of "expansionary fiscal austerity"—the idea that the way out of an economic slump is to cut spending, which will lead to rising business confidence, more investment and strong growth.

Does the austerity doctrine actually make any sense—that is, explain and predict how real economies operate? Mark Blyth's review of economic history in his influential book *Austerity* turns up dozens of examples of the abject failure of austerity economics from the 1920s and 1930s—the examples that led Keynes to formulate his famous theories—to the recent attempts to apply austerity in Europe, where the dire anti-growth effects are currently on display.[25] Counter-examples of successful austerity are few and far between.

The academic literature fares no better, being long on theory and short on solid empirical evidence. Indeed, as Paul Krugman and others have pointed out, one could not ask for a better, cleaner, real-world test of the austerity vs. Keynesian theories than we have had in the last six or seven years. Austerity, as predicted by Keynesian theory, has been a drag on economic recovery from recession, slowing economic growth by subtracting demand from economies and leading in some countries to outright contraction. By and large, the more austerity implemented in a country, the more economic pain suffered and the poorer the country's subsequent growth performance.[26]

Consistent with these relationships, Europe has suffered more than the United States since the Great Financial Crisis because it has implemented more austerity than the United States. In most of these countries, this has had a great deal to do with membership in the 19-country currency union known as the Eurozone. Since the Eurozone is a currency union without any fiscal union (unlike, say, the United States), countries simultaneously have no power to devalue their currency in response to severe economic difficulties and no common fiscal pot from which to draw support. So when things went very bad—as they did for a number of European countries—and borrowing costs to service debt rose to crisis levels, these countries had no recourse but to beg for support from supranational economic authorities (the so-called Troika: the European Commission, the European Central Bank and the International Monetary Fund) and accede to whatever terms were dictated.

These terms were driven by the philosophy, held at least initially by all these authorities and heavily driven by German insistence, that austerity in the cause of "structural reform" must be immediately adopted and followed indefinitely until certain deficit and debt targets are reached. This course, once adopted, would bolster investor confidence and healthy growth would resume in fairly short order, claimed the Troika.

This has, to say the least, not been the case. Neither investor confidence nor healthy growth have returned and, because of continued low or negative growth, high levels of government debt—the ostensible reason why so much austerity was needed—have improved little in these countries or even worsened. Indeed, austerity policy, implemented to a greater or lesser degree throughout the Eurozone, actually managed in 2011 to produce a second recession from which these countries are still recovering. Eurozone real GDP growth was negative in both 2012 and 2013 (–0.9 and –0.3 percent, respectively) and just 0.9 percent in 2014 and 1.7 percent in 2015.[27] And there are countries like Spain, Portugal, Italy and, of course, Greece that, as of early 2016, had yet to recover the GDP level they attained eight years before at the onset of the Great Recession.[28]

Austerity policies have also managed to undermine countries' future growth prospects. In other words, not only are austerity-ridden countries growing slowly now but their future growth paths have been lowered significantly relative to pre-recession trends. On a country-by-country basis, the extent of this damage is closely associated with the amount of austerity administered.[29] So in terms of both short-run and long-run growth payoffs, austerity has been an abject failure.

SECULAR STAGNATION

This last point brings up another policy-dependent problem slowing growth in advanced countries. This is "secular stagnation," the idea that advanced economies have suffered such severe damage to their long-term growth paths that healthy growth is unlikely to return without significant intervention. Current policies, as argued most forcefully by Harvard economist Larry Summers,[30] are simply not capable of restoring robust growth. Monetary policy can only do so much when interest rates are already very low, the private sector is risk-averse and a glut of savings is accumulating. Nor can standard fiscal policies, even if they edge away from austerity, provide enough juice to jump-start the engine. This situation, the argument runs, is not just temporary but could last for a generation or more as low investor expectations, low interest rates and conventional fiscal policy interact to produce long-term stagnation.

The solution, Summers and others say, lies in far more expansionary fiscal policy focused on investment, particularly in infrastructure. More generally, as summarized by Berkeley economist Brad Delong, the threat of long-term stagnation means that government should act as "investment-spender, risk-bearer, safe asset-supplier, and bubble-preventer of last resort, and thus extend its proper role beyond that of Keynesian demand-management policies toward what Keynes called a 'comprehensive socialization of investment.'"[31] Given the very low interest rate environment, governments can afford to take on this expansive role; they can borrow far more than they currently are and invest heavily in infrastructure and maintenance, producing long-term economic benefits that far outweigh the costs of servicing the resultant debt. Indeed, as the

International Monetary Fund—hardly known for its free-spending ways—notes, under current circumstances the long-run effect of such investment on countries' debt burden should be to decrease that burden, not increase it.[32]

So infrastructure investment is, to say the least, a very good deal for today's advanced capitalist countries. And it is a central part of a policy orientation that is not an option but rather a necessity to unlock the growth potential of today's capitalism. The alternative is continued stagnation, with all the economic and social pathologies that that implies. To not grasp this alternative is policy error of the most egregious sort.

FULL EMPLOYMENT

Combatting secular stagnation through expansive fiscal policy is also integral to remedying another policy-dependent problem undermining growth: the failure to run the economy at full employment, where everyone who is willing and able to work can find a job. Full employment was enshrined in the United States as a primary goal of the federal government in the Humphrey-Hawkins Full Employment Act of 1978 and, in a softer form ("maximum sustainable employment"), was made part of the dual mandate of the Federal Reserve (along with price stability) around the same time. Ironically, the record of sustaining full employment has been dreadful since then. In the 1949–79 period, the U.S. economy was at full employment

69 percent of the time; from 1979 to the present day, the economy has been at full employment only 29 percent of the time.[33]

This is because the passage of the Humphrey-Hawkins full employment bill happened to coincide with the conservative economic counter-revolution that attached little significance to full employment as a policy goal. Instead, it was deemed far more important to keep inflation down, lower taxes, remove regulatory inefficiencies and let capitalism find its natural level. If more unemployment resulted, so be it—it would do more harm than good to interfere and risk a spike in inflation.

It is unsurprising that a period when full employment was the exception not the rule has coincided with a period of rapidly escalating inequality. The most straightforward effect of full employment is that it increases employer competition for workers, leading to rising wages, especially at the low end of the labor market. Conversely, the lack of full employment produces slack labor markets where employers call the shots and low-wage workers are particularly disadvantaged. This of course increases inequality, just as we have generally seen since 1979 (with the exception of the 1995–2000 period, a period of—you guessed it—full employment).

This rising inequality in and of itself undermines growth by taking money out of the hands of those most likely to spend, not save, their income. Running the economy at full employment most of the time should partially reverse this trend and boost growth. And full employment forces employers to increase investment and deploy their (now more expensive) workers more efficiently, which should have beneficial effects on productivity and therefore also boost growth.[34]

In short, more full employment means less inequality and more growth. It is policy error, pure and simple, not to promote this outcome and focus only on price stability.

If policy error is holding back growth, why hasn't the left taken up the banner more forthrightly for these growth-promoting measures—jettisoning budget austerity, combatting secular stagnation through infrastructure-fueled fiscal expansion and running the economy persistently at full employment? They are leaving growth on the table, growth which would be beneficial to their emerging postindustrial coalition and cement this coalition's support for the left.

The answer lies in the long slow death of the welfare state and the welfare state coalition as industrial capitalism declined. The mainstream left parties have for several decades been on the defensive and preoccupied with preserving as much as possible of the welfare state against a conservative onslaught fed by industrial decline. With the rapid erosion of the left's traditional coalition and with the postindustrial coalition just taking shape, the left felt its most effective defensive option was to accept the idea that this newest stage of capitalism, more or less unfettered, would produce adequate growth and then press for a reasonably fair distribution of benefits from growth.

That strategy did not work from either a growth or fair distribution perspective. But the left's emerging postindustrial coalitions, which are now quite strong and getting stronger by the year, need more growth and fairer distribution. So left parties, responding to this unmet demand, are becoming more and more open to the idea that capitalism has been under-performing on both growth and fairness. Capitalism can do better with robust government policies and wise investments; equity and growth are not in fact opposed and can work together.

So there is now ideological and political room to correct these policy errors and embark on a higher growth path. This is very clear in the United States, where the Democratic Party and its leading figures, Barack Obama and Hillary Clinton, have been taking stronger and stronger stands against austerity and for ramped-up investment in infrastructure, education, child care and much more. It is less clear in Europe, where the train wreck known as the Eurozone continues to artificially depress growth prospects and the left has been remarkably quiescent in opposing Germany-driven austerity dictates. But as the economic situation in Europe steadily fails to resolve itself and the populist right gains strength, the left is beginning to realize it has no choice but to push for policy changes that might actually promote, as opposed to depress, growth. This will eventually lead the European left down the same path as the U.S. left, along with a continent-wide push to restructure Eurozone/EU rules to support growth.

THE GREEN ECONOMY

Another important reason why the left will be forced to embark on a different, growth-oriented economic path is the necessity of transitioning to a green economy. The left embraces this goal for the very good reason that the future of the planet may depend on it. But the intimate connection of this goal to strong economic growth is frequently missed.

For one thing, the amount of infrastructure and scientific investment that will be necessary to facilitate this transition is immense, exactly the sort of investment that can help combat secular stagnation and promote full employment.[35] Clean energy investments are particularly effective at creating jobs—and relatively good ones.[36] And of course such a program is completely incompatible with austerity economics.

So an effective approach to the clean energy transition both needs and should facilitate strong growth. It is odd that the left does not stress this connection more than it does. This may have something to do with prevalence of anti-growth sentiments in some of the greener parts of the left. These sentiments could not be more misguided.

The basis for these views has been well summarized[37] by technologist Ramez Naam, author of the recent book *The Infinite Resource: The Power of Ideas on a Finite Planet*:

The world is facing incredibly serious natural resource and environmental challenges: Climate change, fresh water depletion, ocean over-fishing, deforestation, air and water pollution, the struggle to feed a planet of billions.

All of these challenges are exacerbated by ever rising demand—over the next 40 years estimates are that demand for fresh water will rise 50%, demand for food will rise 70%, and demand for energy will nearly double—all in the same period that we need to tackle climate change, depletion of rivers and aquifers, and deforestation.[38]

All of these problems are tied in one way or another to economic growth. So, logically, if we want to stop the problems shouldn't we just stop or even reverse economic growth? Naam rejects this logic despite fully embracing the scale of the problems we face. His first reason is that stopping growth would not work morally or practically.

It would not work morally, Naam argues, because most of future growth will benefit people whose living standards are far below those in the developed world. To tell these people to forego the benefits of economic growth, when those in the developed world have already received those benefits, is grossly unfair. As Naam points out:

Roughly one billion people alive today on the planet have access to automobiles, air conditioners, and central heat. The other six billion do not. Two billion lack access to a toilet. One billion lack access to electricity. The bulk of the growth to come over the next few decades—in global

GDP, in energy consumption, in CO2 emissions, in food consumption, in water use—will all come from the developing world. That growth isn't trivial. It isn't about building McMansions or driving SUVs. It is, by and large, growth that reflects the aspirations of billions of people around the world to rise to a level of comfort that nearly everyone in the rich world—even those we consider poor—enjoy. A path forward that doesn't allow room for billions to rise out of poverty and to at least this modicum of comfort is not a very appealing one.[39]

And stopping growth would definitely not work practically. Even if we could stop growth in the developed world, how are we to stop those in the developing world who want to consume more from doing so? Short of enforcing austerity in the developing world, we can't do that.

Naam's second reason is that stopping growth is not necessary. The resources—water, food, energy, etc.—available to humanity greatly outstrip the potential needs of our population, not only today but in the future. The problem lies in accessing those resources in an economically feasible and environmentally sustainable way. That in turn depends on innovation, both technological and economic.

Take energy and, by extension, climate change. The price of solar energy is coming down fast; a watt of solar power today costs only 5 percent of what it cost in 1980. But it's still too expensive to out-compete fossil fuels, even setting aside, for the moment, the storage problem. The solution: massive investment in clean energy R&D (the United States currently invests only $5 billion a year in this, actually less than it invested in the 1980s) *and* a carbon tax to encourage clean energy use and accelerate innovation. As Naam puts it:

> The fundamental driver here is economics. Consumers, businesses, and industry want energy. They need energy. That's true everywhere in the world. And they will buy whatever sort of energy is cheapest. Indeed, if a new source of energy is sufficiently cheaper than the old, consumers will switch their energy consumption from the old to the new.
>
> If we want to win the race against climate change, one thing matters more than all others: make renewable energy (including storage) cheap. Dirt cheap. And do it fast.[40]

Naam makes similar arguments about challenges in the areas of water and food: the solution is not to stop growth but to innovate and to do it fast. In this, he joins such "green growth" advocates as Ralf Fücks, president of the Heinrich Böll Foundation and a leading member of the German Green Party, whose new book *Green Growth, Smart Growth* lays out a number of ideas similar to Naam's.[41] This is indicative of a new attitude toward economic growth among much of the green left in advanced countries.

IN DEFENSE OF TECHNO-OPTIMISM

Of course, Naam's views may be rejected by some on the left because he is unabashedly a techno-optimist. Well, what's wrong with that? The fact of the matter is that almost everything people like about the modern world, including relatively high living standards, is traceable to technological advances and the knowledge embodied in those advances. From smart phones, flat screen TVs and the internet to air and auto travel to central heating and air conditioning to the medical devices and drugs that cure disease and extend life to electric lights and the mundane flush toilet—the list is endless—technology has dramatically transformed people's lives, making them both much better and much longer than they ever have been before. It is difficult to argue that the average person today is not far, far better off than her counterpart in the past. As the Northwestern University economic historian Joel Mokyr puts it, the so-called good old days were old but they were not good.[42]

And what do we have to thank for all these spectacular advances? Technology! Technology has both enabled the new goods, machines, medicine and so on that we consume and enabled the economic growth that allows us to consume at such a high level. Of course, economists debate endlessly about the exact mechanisms connecting technology to growth and what social and institutional conditions must be met for technology to maximize its effect on growth, but at the end of the day the growth we have seen—and the living standards we enjoy—would simply not have been possible without the massive breakthroughs and continuous improvements we have seen in the technological realm.

Given all this and given the central importance of economic growth to the left's prospects, one would think that the left would embrace techno-optimism rather than shying away from it. After all, if the goal is to be successful and improve people's lives, rapid technological advance is surely something to promote enthusiastically. But the left has been oddly circumspect about the possibilities of new and better technologies, allowing the techno-optimism space to be dominated by libertarian-minded denizens of Silicon Valley.[43] As British science journalist Leigh Phillips puts it:

> Once upon a time, the left . . . promised more innovation, faster progress, *greater abundance*. One of the reasons I believe that the historically fringe ideology of libertarianism is today so surprisingly popular in Silicon Valley and with tech-savvy young people more broadly . . . is that libertarianism is the only extant ideology that so substantially promises a significantly materially better future.[44]

There are several reasons for the left's ambiguous relationship to technology. One has already been mentioned: the left has tended to underestimate the importance of economic growth in the recent past, believing incorrectly that they can achieve their social objectives in an era of a tepid and poorly distributed growth. That leads naturally to an under-estimation of the importance of technological change, since one of its chief attributes is promoting growth.

Second, and worse, many on the left tend to regard tech-nological change with dread rather than hope. They see technology as a force facilitating inequality rather than growth, disadvantaging manual workers rather than lead-ing to skilled job creation, turning consumers into corpo-rate pawns rather than information-savvy citizens and destroying the planet in the process. We are far, far away from the traditional left attitude that welcomed technolog-ical change as the handmaiden of abundance and increased leisure. Or, for that matter, from the liberal optimism that permeated the culture of the 1950s and '60s with tantaliz-ing visions of flying cars and obedient robots.

Third, the left has become infected with general pessi-mism about prospects for growth, acceding, as we have seen, to the idea that growth can't really be much greater than it already is. Just as this devalues the role of policy it also devalues the role of technological change. Why be op-timistic about technological change if it's not likely to have much effect anyway?

Feeding right into these sentiments is the growth of academic techno-pessimism. The leading light in this emerging school of thought is economist Robert Gordon, coincidentally in the same department at Northwestern

University where leading techno-optimist Mokyr teaches. In his 2012 paper, "Is Economic Growth Over?: Faltering Innovation Confronts the Six Headwinds," and then in a number of follow-up papers and a massive book, Gordon argues that economic growth on the level we've been used to in the last 200 years may in fact be a historical anomaly and that strong growth has only been possible because of dramatic new innovations that have turbocharged economic advance—"industrial revolutions" in his terminology.[45] The first industrial revolution was 1750–1830, based around steam engines, cotton spinning and railroads. The second revolution was 1870–1900, featuring electricity, the internal combustion engine and running water with indoor plumbing. He believes that both these industrial revolutions took about 100 years to work their way through the economy and generate their full effects. For example, the second industrial revolution was still giving us advances like air conditioning, home appliances and the interstate highway system in the 1950–70 period.

The third industrial revolution is centered on computers and the internet. Gordon is not impressed with this revolution. He thinks all the really important, transformative stuff came from the first two revolutions, especially the second. He is fond of posing this question in his public lectures: which would you be willing to give up, your iPhone or the flush toilet?

He thinks the post-1970 slowdown in productivity growth (it dropped by about half) is traceable to the relative triviality of the computer/internet revolution. And when we finally got a burst of productivity growth in the 1996–2004 period, it quickly petered out. The reason, he believes, is that the third industrial revolution has already run out of gas (no 100-year phase-in here) and just doesn't have much more to give us. Because of this and because of his six "headwinds" to growth (demographic burdens, stagnating educational attainment, high levels of inequality, globalization, rising energy and environmental costs, and high levels of household and government debt), he projects an ongoing decline in per capita economic growth to a meager 0.2 percent per year this century.

But is it really true that all the cool stuff has already been invented? This does not seem likely. Mokyr points to emerging fields of innovation such as 3-D printing, genetic modification and custom-designed materials.[46] There is also the rapid development of self-driving cars and ever-more sophisticated robots and artificial intelligence systems. Even more significantly, technology related to the generation and storage of clean energy has been advancing by leaps and bounds. For example, the price of solar power has been declining exponentially for years; according to Naam, the price of electricity from new solar declines by about 16 percent every time solar capacity doubles.[47] And progress has also been extremely rapid in making battery storage of renewable energy inexpensive, reliable and large-scale. Surely cheap, renewable energy qualifies as a breakthrough innovation.

More generally, it is worth noting that by the end of the twentieth century more technological advances had been made in the previous hundred years than in all of history before 1900. As physicist Michio Kaku argues in his book *Visions: How Science Will Revolutionize the 21st Century,* there is no good reason to believe that this breakneck pace will slow in the twenty-first century, since we are just on the verge of mastering knowledge gleaned from technological revolutions in three interwined areas: computer science, biomolecular science/engineering, and quantum physics.[48] Indeed, as we transition from an era where we have discovered the basic laws and building blocks in these fields to an era where we apply that knowledge, the pace of innovation, if anything, may accelerate. Currently underdeveloped fields like biotechnology, nanotechnology and quantum computing may leap forward in ways we cannot exactly anticipate but that are likely to have a big impact.

Rather than correctly predicting a long-term innovation slowdown, it seems more likely that Gordon and his co-thinkers will join the long list of economic pessimists that have been proven wrong over the last 150 years.[49] As blogger Kevin Drum cogently puts it:

> I can somehow imagine a circa-1870 version of Gordon arguing that all this folderol about electricity is ridiculous. Why, we've been studying electricity for over a century, and what do we have to show for it? Some clunky batteries, the telegraph, a few arc lamps with limited use,

and a steady supply of techno-optimist inventors who keep telling us that any day now they'll invent a practical generator that will replace steam engines and change the world. Don't believe it, folks.[50]

Interestingly, Drum, despite his bracing critique, is himself a sort of techno-pessimist—or, more precisely, a pessimistic techno-optimist. In an influential article for *Mother Jones* magazine, provocatively titled "Welcome Robot Overlords: Please Don't Fire Us?" Drum envisions robots growing smarter and more capable at an exponential rate so that by, say 2040, there will not be much need for human workers.[51] Result: mass unemployment and social dysfunction despite unprecedented technological advance.

Thus Drum goes to the other extreme from Gordon. Not only will there not be an innovation slowdown but there will be such a drastic innovation speedup that it will put everybody out of work. But this is just as unrealistic as Gordon. As Anthony Carnevale and Stephen Rose point out in their detailed study of the technological transformation of the U.S. economy, instead of assuming a virtual vanishing of growth as Gordon does, Drum is implicitly assuming economic growth in the neighborhood of 10 percent per year as smart machines generate greater and greater output without human intervention.[52]

This seems unlikely to say the least. Yet this point of

view is not without influence on the left, where a sort of neo-Luddism has become increasingly common. Drum himself has remarked: "The Luddites weren't wrong. They were just 200 years too early."[53] Martin Ford's 2015 book, *Rise of the Robots: Technology and the Threat of a Jobless Future*, which predicts half of U.S. workers will be replaced by robots in the next 20 years, was widely and respectfully reviewed in liberal outlets.[54] Coming after a spell of high unemployment from the Great Recession, which is just lifting in the United States (and still hasn't in much of Europe), this seems like a very odd thing for those on the left to worry about. It is especially odd when the history of technological advance is full of transformations that put workers out of jobs in one sector only to have more jobs created in others as demand for new products and services grew.[55]

It's time for the left to discard both the Gordon and Drum forms of techno-pessimism and firmly embrace techno-optimism. Continuing technological advance is not only probable but good; instead of a future of no jobs it will be a future of different and more highly skilled jobs. These advances will likely transform our lives dramatically—in some ways we can already see and some we cannot anticipate. They will be a key to human liberation and critically to the growth that will facilitate the pursuit of social justice and a higher standard of living for all. Techno-optimism is too important to be left to the libertarians.

GLOBALIZATION IS A FORCE FOR GOOD

Another area where the left falls down is its attitude toward globalization. This is often hostile—trade costs jobs, especially manufacturing jobs; global competition destroys the economic base of local communities; rising nations like China are undercutting us with cheap labor and unfair trading practices; international capital seeks lower wages and looser regulation everywhere, promoting a race to the bottom; and so on. This casts globalization as an enemy of healthy growth and the ordinary worker and therefore something that should be opposed by the left.

This attitude is misguided on several levels. First, globalization has been central to the economic advances that have dramatically raised living standards all over the world. Indeed, most parts of the developing world have made huge progress in the last half century as globalization has bound countries closer and closer together. Because of this, the proportion of the world's population that lives on less than 2,200 calories a day has fallen from 56 percent in the mid-1960s to less than 10 percent today. The proportion of the world's population living in "extreme poverty" (currently defined by the World Bank as under $1.90 a day) has fallen from 44 percent in 1981 to less than 10 percent today.[56] Put in terms of absolute numbers, there were almost 2 billion people living in extreme poverty in 1990; that is down to around 700 million today. That means around a quarter of the world's population has been lifted out of extreme poverty in just the last 25 years—25 years that have coincided with an acceleration of globalization.

This trend has been strongest in East Asia, especially China, but it has greatly affected all parts of the developing world, including Sub-Saharan Africa, frequently the poster child for the alleged failures of globalization. In Sub-Saharan Africa, the percent of the population living in extreme poverty has dropped from 56 percent in 1990 to 35 percent today. More broadly, as Branko Milanovic, one of the world's leading scholars on income distribution, notes:

> Global income distribution [since the fall of the Berlin Wall] has changed in a remarkable way. It was probably the most profound global reshuffle of people's economic positions since the Industrial Revolution. Broadly speaking the bottom third . . . became significantly better off and many of the people there escaped absolute poverty. The middle third or more became much richer, seeing their real incomes rise by approximately 3 per cent per capita annually.[57]

Accompanying these dramatic rises in income have been dramatic increases in health. Between 1990 and 2013, the percentage of the world's children who died before their fifth birthday fell by almost half.[58] And overall life expectancy continues to climb, reaching 70 for those born in 2011. Back in 1950 world life expectancy was only 47. The average Mexican today lives longer than the average Briton did in 1955.[59] And stunningly, of all the people in human history who have reached the age of 65, half are alive today.[60]

These are amazing advances and they are taking place while the world is becoming ever more globalized. That's because globalization, far from driving a race to the bottom, makes possible (even if it does not guarantee uniform progress in every country at every time) the spread of material progress to every corner of the earth. Marx, despite his underestimation of capitalism's long-run potential, understood this.[61] The broad left throughout most of the twentieth century understood this. But many on today's left have lost track of this fundamental truth and prefer instead to focus on the obvious facts that globalization has some negative effects, both in developing and advanced countries, and that material progress has been very uneven. But it is only this maddening, uneven, unfair process that makes serious economic progress for most of the human race possible. Therefore, on ethical and moral grounds alone, the left should enthusiastically embrace globalization, even as they seek to mitigate its negative effects where they occur and spread its benefits more evenly.

Some on the left are willing to grant that globalization has raised living standards in the developing world but insist that it is the enemy of the developed world worker, due above all to the destruction of manufacturing jobs. But is this really true? As noted in chapter two, the decline of industrial employment is a very long-run trend that predates the sharp rise in globalization toward the end of the last century. And, if you plot the share of manufacturing jobs specifically in overall U.S. employment since 1948, there has been a steady decline from a high of about 35 percent to less than 10 percent today, with recent declines no sharper than those that have occurred in the past.[62]

There is a very simple reason for this. Much of the decline in manufacturing employment can be traced to rapidly rising productivity in the manufacturing sector—so the same output could be produced with fewer workers—combined with shifts in demand toward services, reflecting a rise in consumer affluence. In this sense, declining manufacturing employment was an inevitable product of capitalism's evolution.

Now that does not mean that globalization has played *no* role in declining manufacturing employment or that foreign trade has no negative effects. Academic studies generally acknowledge some "trade effect" on manufacturing jobs.[63] Moreover, trade with China in particular has probably had a significant recent impact.[64] It is also likely that job loss from trade is larger in cyclical downturns, when economic vulnerability among workers is particularly high. But it does mean that attributing the massive, long-term decline in manufacturing jobs across the advanced world to globalization is a stretch.

More broadly, attempts to blame globalization for the wage and income problems of workers in advanced countries ignore hugely important factors like capitalism's Piketty problem, the advance of the right and serial policy error, as sketched in this chapter and earlier. Clearly, the globalization explanation does not go very far in explaining the totality of workers' problems today.

The point about policy error is key. The left will do a lot more good by correcting policy error on growth, employment and fiscal policy than by standing in the way of globalization. This even applies to the specifics of the manufacturing jobs issue. Germany, for example, has recently done far better than the United States in moderating manufacturing job loss by retraining manufacturing workers from import-competing industries and moving them into export-oriented manufacturing jobs.[65]

In short, globalization is not the villain many on the left make it out to be. It is simply part of the way capitalism today works and will increasingly work in the future. The sensible response is not to denounce it but to make it work for as large a share of the population as possible. This can be done by embracing globalization as a potential agent of growth and prosperity, rather than stagnation and job loss.

The key to doing this is recognizing that globalization is not a zero-sum game, where the developing world's gain is the developed world's loss. Instead, it is a positive sum game where increased prosperity in the developing world and denser trade ties should mean increased prosperity in the developed world through larger markets for developed countries' goods and services and potential infusions of foreign human and investment capital. Therefore, in addition to the equitable growth and full employment policies outlined earlier, the left should concentrate on ensuring that workers dislocated by globalization can move smoothly into other economic sectors and that openness in developed countries' economies is matched by openness in developing countries' economies. Ultimately, more wealth and a better life in the developing world should mean the same in the developed world. In short, it is time for the typical leftist to discard their jaundiced view of global capitalism's potential and embrace their inner optimist. The time of "the optimistic leftist"—the subject of the next chapter—is upon us.

FOUR

The Optimistic Leftist

Why is today's left so pessimistic? One reason is that inequality has been rising for decades and the left has not succeeded in stopping it. This promotes a sense that the left is losing ground and is likely to lose further ground in the future.

Another is that an era when mass left political parties enjoyed great electoral success (pre-1970s) has been succeeded by an era in which success has been far harder to come by, even when capitalism was on the ropes in the aftermath of the Great Financial Crisis. Pessimistic leftists look at this and despair.

Perhaps even more important is the feeling that problems like global warming and resource depletion are so big and so advanced that the left has little chance of solving them in time. It is five minutes to midnight and the clock is ticking. Pessimism, in this view, is only realism.

Then there is the fact that, with socialism off the table as an alternative form of economic organization, we appear to be stuck with capitalism, warts and all. For some leftists, those warts are so severe that all we can really hope for now is to contain the damage. That's a depressing prospect.

But this is all wrong. In fact, capitalism can be made to work better, in fact much better, and the problems we face can and will be solved. That's the left's job and it is entirely feasible. But to do so the left first needs to realize that their pessimism about the state of the world today and its future is profoundly mistaken.

PESSIMISM IS NEITHER USEFUL NOR JUSTIFIED

It is mistaken for two very important reasons. The first is that pessimism is an absolutely terrible selling point. As explained in the first chapter, pessimism is fundamentally demobilizing, not mobilizing. If things were terrible yesterday, are worse today and are likely to get even worse tomorrow, this does not motivate the typical person to engage in heroic struggle to change the world. It is more likely to make her or him cautious, guarded and determined to hold on to what little they have. Thus by wallowing—seemingly with relish—in a slough of despond about the state of the world, the left only manages to undercut its ability to mobilize ordinary people for positive change.

Optimism, by contrast, mobilizes people. It allows people to raise their heads from the daily struggle for existence, envision something better and believe it's actually possible to get there. That makes the project of joining together with others to make positive change seem worth the effort it typically entails. There will likely be a payoff to such effort, not just a return to square one or worse, as a pessimistic stance implies.

The second reason is that the substantive case for pessimism is simply wrong. It is optimism, not pessimism, that is securely rooted in the facts about social evolution and economic change. Here are the basic details of the case for optimism.

Start with the lives people lead today compared to those they led in the past. As noted in the previous chapter, world poverty has declined dramatically over time. A little less than 200 years ago, in 1820, the estimated world extreme poverty rate was 84 percent;[1] it is now down to single digits. The UN estimates that poverty has been reduced by more in the last 50 years than in the previous 500. By the decade of the 2030s, the world extreme poverty rate may well approach zero.

This trend is part of a long-range shift that has transformed world society, starting in the seventeenth century. In that century, world GDP per capita rose about 16 percent, followed by another 19 percent rise in the eighteenth century.

Then, with the nineteenth century, the GDP per capita growth rate exploded to around 250 percent, followed by a stunning, nearly 900 percent growth rate in the twentieth century.[2] Based on current growth trends, by the time the current century is over, the average per capita income across the entire world should be half again as high as it is in the world's most advanced country, the United States, today.[3]

Of course, there's more to material progress than just incomes. But judging by non-monetary metrics, the changes have been even more spectacular. Consider life expectancy. As also noted in the previous chapter, life expectancy is way up all over the world. Even in an advanced country like England, the average life expectancy was just 37 in 1748, 38 in 1849, and 46 in 1900, but reached 78 by 2000.[4] Across the world, life expectancy has doubled since 1800, even as population has increased six-fold.[5]

Then there is how people live those longer lives. The decline of punishing manual labor and debilitating disease is well known. But progress goes far beyond that.[6] In the United States today, 99 percent of poor people have running water, electricity and flush toilets, 95 percent have a television, 88 percent a telephone, 71 percent a car and 70 percent air conditioning.[7] Reaction to these facts may well be: "of course, how could it be any different?" Yet these are all things that the fabulously wealthy nineteenth-century robber baron Cornelius Vanderbilt lacked. And these great advances leave out cheap consumer electronics and the internet—an explosion of information, connectivity and entertainment available to larger and larger segments of the U.S. and world population.

There's also less violence in those longer lives (one reason why those lives are longer).[8] Despite the horrendous wars of the twentieth century, the death toll per capita was still far lower than it was in our supposedly idyllic past. Indeed, if the warfare death rate of hunter-gatherer societies had prevailed in the twentieth century, we would have had 2 billion war-related deaths rather than 100 million,[9] not to mention the high rates of torture and enslavement that would have gone along with them.

The economic progress underpinning these positive developments has been driven by at least four underlying trends: increased educational levels, technological innovation, increased economic interconnectedness and the rise of mixed capitalist economies that facilitate both growth and a more egalitarian distribution of its fruits. Could these trends continue? Absolutely. Educational levels around the globe have been rising at a startling rate for a long time and show no signs of stopping. In the United States, adults' average years of schooling has risen from 2 years in 1820 to 6 in 1870, 8 in 1920, 10 in 1960 and around 13 today.[10] Globally, just since 1970, the illiteracy rate has dropped from 44 to 17 percent.[11] In the same time period, the proportion of the relevant global population enrolled in tertiary education (some form of college) has risen from 10 to 33 percent.[12]

As for technological advance, as explained in the previous chapter, the concept that we have come to the end of significant technological progress is not credible. Far more likely is economic historian Joel Mokyr's take that "we ain't seen nothing yet."[13] We don't know exactly where or when the next waves of technological transformation will come, but come they will.

On economic interconnectedness, the increasingly thorough integration of the BRIC nations (Brazil, Russia, India, China) is bringing 42 percent of the world's population into close contact with the world economy. And the overall process of globalization shows no signs of slowing down. Since 1950, the volume of world trade has increased 27 fold, three times faster than world output.[14] Exports as a percentage of GDP have tripled over the same period.[15] The weight of trade in the world economy now far exceeds levels reached at any point in the past, including the classical free-trade period of the late 1800s and early 1900s.

In terms of mixed economies, the last several decades has seen the profound transformation of almost all planned economies to some sort of mixed capitalist economy. Some of these countries (e.g., China) retain considerable state control but the shift toward market capitalism is nevertheless undeniable. The mixed economy has become dominant across the world and, based on its track record, should become even more so over time.

Finally, an overarching trend has facilitated all these trends and lays the basis for their continuance: the rise of democracy and human rights. It wasn't so long ago that democracy was an unusual way to run a political system;

today it is quite common. The number of countries with some form of democracy has more than doubled since 1980 and almost quintupled since 1950.[16] And preference for basic democratic rights, including for women, is now almost universal among the world's population.[17]

What applies globally applies even more for the advanced countries, where living standards are many multiples of what they were a hundred years ago, literacy is universal, the mixed economy has been most successful and democracy and human rights have achieved their highest expression yet. And it is where the role of the left has been most obvious in propelling human progress forward.

Start with democracy itself. As Geoff Eley notes in his magisterial *Forging Democracy: The History of the Left in Europe*, the left in its original incarnation around the French Revolution

> became identified with a strong democratic stance embracing abolition of the royal veto, single-chamber legislature, an elected rather than an appointed judiciary, legislative supremacy rather than separation of powers and a strong executive, and—most vital of all— the democratic franchise of one man, one vote.[18]

As the left progressed through the nineteenth century, the fight for ever-wider democracy was central to its raison d'etre and the area of many of its greatest victories. It is worth noting that free, universal, secret, adult and equal suffrage, wedded to freedoms of press, association, speech, etc.—which is today considered the essence of democracy—did not exist, even in advanced countries, until the twentieth century. It took a long, hard struggle, led by the left, to finally get there.

More broadly, when we think of the many very important ways advanced societies have progressed over the years, the role of the left is prominent in nearly all of them. For example, in the United States, the broad left has played an essential role in achieving the following:

- The 8-hour workday and 40-hour workweek
- Worker's compensation for on-the-job accidents
- Unemployment insurance
- Prohibitions against child labor and workplace exploitations
- The legal right of people to organize within labor unions and engage in collective bargaining for fair wages and benefits
- The constitutional right to vote for women
- The graduated income and inheritance tax
- Protections against contaminated food and medicines
- Hundreds of millions of acres of protected wilderness areas, waterways and national parks
- Anti-monopoly and pro-competitive regulations of corporations

- Direct elections of U.S. senators, direct primary elections of political candidates, the initiative and referendum process in the states
- Civil service tests to replace political patronage
- National supervision of banks and the creation of a flexible national currency
- Regulation of the securities industry
- Federal insurance of bank deposits
- Bans on speculative banking practices
- Refinancing and foreclosure protections for home and farm owners
- National infrastructure including electrification, railways, airports, bridges and roads, and broadband development
- Social Security and Medicare to aid the elderly and Medicaid and CHIP to help low-income families and children
- Minimum-wage laws and income support for the working poor
- Public education, college loans and grants for students, and the G.I. Bill.[19]

Similar lists can easily be compiled for other advanced countries. They all show that the left has been repeatedly successful in advancing democracy, improving living conditions and promoting healthy, inclusive capitalist growth.

The last point deserves to be stressed. The left's greatest creation may be the mixed economy, which has combined market capitalism with financial regulation; automatic stabilizers for boom and bust cycles; effective public health measures; a vast expansion of public and publicly financed education from elementary school to college; huge public investments in infrastructure, from the canals and railroads of the nineteenth century to the highways, airways and electric and telecommunications grids of the twentieth; support of basic research leading to technological breakthroughs; and much more. It's not just that the mixed economy has made capitalism more humane—it has had a central role in enabling capitalism to make the fantastic strides it has made in the last 150 years.

This point used to be widely understood—indeed consensual across advanced societies. But the years since 1970 have seen a great forgetting of this essential point, particularly in the United States. Political scientists Jacob Hacker and Paul Pierson term this remarkable development "American Amnesia" in their recent book analyzing the growth of American prosperity. [20] Of course, the conservative movement has played a leading role in promoting this amnesia, but, as Hacker and Pierson note, good chunks of the left have been complicit in this amnesia (though this is beginning to change).

THE GREAT REVERSAL?

So it would seem that the left has considerable grounds for optimism based on the historical record. But wait—don't the developments of the last 40 years completely undermine this optimistic case? Sure, maybe optimism was once justified, but not anymore—nothing good has happened for decades thanks to the conservatives, the big money guys and the general rapaciousness of contemporary capitalism. This is a claim supported by a seemingly endless stream of books and articles documenting how awful things have gotten. Representative titles include Donald Bartlett's and James Steele's *America: What Went Wrong?*, Hedrick Smith's *Who Stole the American Dream?* and Robert Putnam's *Our Kids: The American Dream in Crisis*. A slightly less histrionic European counterpart is Tony Judt's *Ill Fares the Land*.[21] Don't these and other books have it right? Hasn't progress essentially stopped—in fact, been reversed?

Wrong again! Looking at the American case, where rhetoric is perhaps the most heated, there is certainly much to complain about today, from grotesquely high levels of inequality to decaying infrastructure to the still potent aftereffects of the Great Recession. Indeed, a central argument of this book is that a much better American society is an eminently attainable goal. However, quite a few left commentators seem to think that "better" means "just like the good ol' days." Holding up American society of 50 or 60 years ago as a model society appears to be particularly in vogue, judging from the writings referenced above.

This is sentimental hogwash. The era of the 1950s or 1960s was in no sense an idyllic progressive past, and it does violence to the task of envisioning a better future to assume otherwise. A good example of this mistaken nostalgia can be found in the Putnam book cited above. Putnam provides a depressing portrayal of what has happened to his hometown of Port Clinton, Ohio, since 1959, the year that he graduated from high school. According to Putnam, it's been pretty much all downhill for Port Clinton for the past five decades. What was once a vibrant community where well-paying jobs were widely available in the local factory, where high school students could aspire to an affordable college education and middle-class lifestyle regardless of their class background, and where, above all, people cared for one another has been gradually destroyed by the closing of the factory that was the town's major employer, lack of job opportunities, growing economic inequality and the decline of any sense of shared fate or common purpose.

Putnam's central thesis is that the story of Port Clinton is the story of America over the past fifty years. The loss of well-paying blue-collar jobs, growing economic inequality and a declining sense of common purpose have turned the American dream into something closer to an American nightmare for most people. It's a tale that undoubtedly rings true to many who have tried making it in post–financial collapse America.

There is no doubt that many Americans have been suffering from the effects of high unemployment and stagnant wages in recent years and that small factory towns like Port Clinton have been especially hard hit. But a closer look at the evidence shows that Putnam's portrayal of fifties- and sixties-era American society as a land of economic opportunity and common purpose is one-sided at best and that, in many respects, America today is a much better, more open, more just and considerably more affluent society.

Incredibly, Putnam's nearly rhapsodic portrayal of past American life completely ignores the pervasive effects of racism, sexism and religious bigotry. He briefly mentions the two African American students in his graduating class who managed to overcome racial prejudice and go on to graduate from college and attend graduate school. But very few African American students in the 1950s were so fortunate. The vast majority attended inferior segregated schools and could look forward to menial jobs traditionally reserved for blacks if they could find jobs at all. Only about one in five would even graduate from high school and less than one in twenty would graduate from college.[22] And in the southern states, where the large majority of African Americans lived, segregation backed by intimidation and, when necessary, violence, was still horrifyingly omnipresent. Very few black people could vote, or eat in the same restaurants or stay in the same hotels as white people.

The most egregious aspects of this appalling system were dismantled in the 1960s. But it is important to stress that progress continued after that. In 1970, just 5 percent of blacks 25 and older had a four-year college degree and only 34 percent had even graduated from high school. Today the analogous figures are 22 percent and 85 percent.[23] The black middle and upper class have expanded dramatically over time; according to Pew Research, 57 percent of black households today qualify as middle or upper class.[24]

Changes in the realm of public opinion are quite dramatic. Opposition to discrimination, approval of interracial dating and marriage and willingness to vote for qualified blacks to be president are essentially universal views among Americans.[25]

Of course, much remains to be done. There are still large economic and educational gaps between blacks (and Hispanics) and whites and areas of concentrated poverty are still distressingly common among the former groups. The criminal justice system, both in terms of policing practices and mass incarceration, is a particularly vexing locus of continued problems for black Americans, as the Black Lives Matter movement has forcefully emphasized. But none of this means that great progress hasn't been made. It simply means there is still far to go.

Women, too, faced a hostile environment in the supposedly "idyllic" past if they aspired to any career other than mother and housewife. Women were only about half as likely as men to graduate from college until after 1970.[26] If they managed to matriculate, the careers open to women were generally limited to traditional female occupations such as nursing and teaching, which paid far less than those reserved for men. Female doctors, lawyers, college professors and business executives were almost unheard of and employment discrimination against women was essentially legal until banned by Title 7 of the 1964 Civil Rights Act.

But since 1970, women's college educational attainment has skyrocketed, quadrupling to 32 percent of the 25-and-older female population.[27] This trend should continue since college attendance and completion rates are increasingly skewed toward women. More young women are attending college than young men right now: 56 percent of today's undergraduates are women, compared to 44 percent who are men.[28] Women now earn around 200,000 more bachelor's degrees each year than men do.[29] Women also now receive more doctoral degrees than men and almost half of new doctors and lawyers are women.[30]

Here too changes in the realm of public opinion have been dramatic. Again, we now have basically unanimous agreement that there should be no discrimination against women or barriers to their achievement, including the highest levels of professional and political attainment and that, moreover, women are equally capable of such achievement.[31] Now there may still be some debate as to the desirability of women's labor force participation when children are present (the so-called mommy wars) but the idea that women should not be able to work if they wish is simply not credible any more. And, as with racial bias, it is hardly the case that gender bias has disappeared. But the magnitude of progress has been remarkable.

It would be hard to overstate the historical degree of bias against gay Americans. Perspectives did not even begin to change until the late 1960s. Not only were homosexual relationships illegal in almost all states back then, but LGBT Americans who came out of the closet, or were forced out, risked losing their jobs and being blacklisted for future employment. Attitudes toward homosexuality in general and toward gay individuals in particular have radically liberalized since then, the most recent manifestation of which was the legalization of gay marriage across the country by the Supreme Court. Of course, biases against gays remain but the rapidity of change in attitudes has been nothing short of spectacular.

The environment is another area of huge progress. *Silent Spring* by Rachel Carson, the book on environmental damage generally credited with kindling the environmental movement, was published only in 1962, and both the Environmental Protection Agency and the first Earth Day date from 1970. Because we are now so used to having a fairly clean environment in terms of air and water quality, it is easy to forget just how far we have come since those times. Rivers and lakes back then were far more likely to be polluted and essentially unsafe for human activity than not; the Cuyahoga River in Cleveland famously caught fire in 1969. But since that era, water quality has improved dramatically; the number of water bodies meeting standard quality criteria has roughly doubled.[32] Icons of pollution, such as Boston Harbor, have been cleaned up. And everywhere towns and cities are investing in waterfront leisure developments that would have been a tasteless joke a generation ago.

Air quality too has increased dramatically. Between 1970 and 2014, emissions of the six key air pollutants that impact public health—ozone, particulate matter, carbon monoxide, nitrogen dioxide, sulfur dioxide and lead—were cut by 69 percent, even as GNP increased by 238 percent.[33] Acid rain has declined by two-thirds.[34] Smog is down by about a third and places like Los Angeles, which had been the smog capital of the United States, now have relatively healthful air. In 1979, when Barack Obama was attending school there and, according to his recollection, experiencing smog constantly, the area had 234 days when the air exceeded current Federal standards for ozone levels.[35] In 2013, the area had only 90 such days. There have been no stage 1 smog alerts (the least serious alert) since 2003, no stage 2 alerts since 1988 and no stage 3 alerts since 1974.

These are all areas that represent tremendous success for the values and priorities of the left in the post-1970 period. Surely the fact that progress has been slower in some other important areas should not blind the left to areas where progress has been substantial. It is time the left learned how to take "yes" for an answer.

UNEQUAL GROWTH AND LIVING STANDARDS

The most obvious objection to this line of argument has to do with the slow growth and heightened inequality that bedeviled advanced societies in the last quarter of the twentieth century and in many ways has worsened since the beginning of the twenty-first. As has been discussed in earlier chapters, it is a fact that economic performance has been relatively poor over this period. This is indeed the main thing that needs to—and will be—fixed, leading to a new era of robust left advance. But it is also true that over this period, around four decades, there has certainly been continued, albeit much slower, economic progress, not a Marxian-style immiseration of the proletariat.

Start with the basic measure of a society's affluence, GDP per capita. Per capita GDP in the United States rose by 111 percent between 1947 and 1979. Between 1979 and 2007 (the last business cycle peak) growth was slower, but per capita GDP still rose by 67 percent over the time period—obviously, the United States became a much richer society over those years, despite the slower growth.[36]

Of course, as has been discussed, this growth has been very unequally distributed, so the effect of this growth on living standards has been much more modest than that suggested by the substantial increase in GDP per capita. The starkest measure of this are the figures for growth of family income from the Census Current Population Survey (CPS).[37] In the 1947–79 period, median family income went up 113 percent, closely matching the gain in GDP per capita over the time period. But in the 1979–2007 period, median family income grew from around $56,000 to $66,000 (2011 dollars), a gain of only 18 percent.[38] Obviously, this lags far behind the growth of GDP per capita over the same time period. On the other hand, it is a gain of nearly a fifth—modest in comparative terms but not nothing and certainly not backsliding.

Moreover, the CPS data do not take into account the changing size of households, the value of non-cash benefits (food stamps, employer-provided health insurance, etc.) and changes in the tax structure. Thus—and there are endless arguments about this among economists—the CPS data may underestimate the gain in living standards over time.[39] Indeed, once all that is taken into account, the Congressional Budget Office (CBO) found that real (inflation-adjusted) after-tax income for the median household grew 50 percent between 1979 and 2007.[40] Again, even this figure lags behind the growth of GDP per capita and is short measure compared to the 314 percent increase for the top 1 percent—but it is far from nothing. Even if one splits the difference between the CPS and CBO figures—in effect, assuming some of the CBO income is not as important as the unadjusted cash income measured by CPS—that would still give median income growth of 34 percent between 1979 and 2007. This is disappointing by historical standards but is far from the miserable picture embraced by many on the left. As the Pew Research Center notes, 84 percent of today's adults have family incomes above what their parents had at similar ages.[41]

Also lost in the standard tale of middle-class decline is the fact that life cycle improvements in living standards have not been repealed by the relatively poor post-1979 environment. That is, it is still the case that as people age, they and their families typically become substantially better off. For example, economist Stephen Rose studied the same individuals as captured by the longitudinal Panel Survey of Income Dynamics and found that 20- to 31-year-olds in 1979 experienced a median growth rate of 56 percent in their income as they aged to 48–59 by 2007.[42]

Speaking of the middle class, this can be another source of definitional dispute between researchers. It is quite possible, for example, for the middle class under some definitions to become smaller even as there is considerable upward mobility from the middle class. This is demonstrated by a 2015 report from the Pew Research Center.[43] According to Pew's definition of the middle class—those with size-adjusted household incomes between two-thirds to double the median—the middle class shrank from 61 percent of adults to 50 percent in the 1971–2015 period. However, most of that shrinkage was due to an increase in the share of adults who were in the upper-middle or highest classes (up 7 points) rather than an increase in the share of adults who were in the lower-middle or lowest classes (up 4 points). So the middle class, under their definition, did shrink, but primarily because of upward, not downward, mobility.

Another excessively gloomy claim about the last several decades is that middle-class jobs are disappearing and being replaced by "McJobs." However, this view equates the decline of low-skill, relatively well-paid jobs like those in manufacturing—which has been going on since 1948—to an overall decline in middle-class jobs, which is not merited. The middle-class jobs of today, as explained in chapter two, are in the growth areas of offices and high-skill services. These two areas of the economy now provide 64 percent of all jobs and have expanded more as a share of jobs since 1967 than manufacturing and related jobs have declined. Thus, middle-class jobs are not disappearing but have rather have moved to new sectors that require higher levels of education and cognitive training.

When thinking about progress in living standards it is also important to keep in mind the ways life has improved for most Americans that are not reflected in income or jobs data.[44] For example, American life expectancy has gone up five years since 1979. Homes are far bigger (median new home size has risen from 1,600 to 2,600 square feet since 1979) and more well-appointed; food and clothing are cheaper and take up a smaller proportion of family budgets; cars are safer and get better gas mileage; access to travel and leisure, including foreign travel, has gone up; and device-enabled connection to the internet has brought the typical American into contact with a universe of information and entertainment that was literally unthinkable 30 or 40 years ago.

The argument that progress has slowed but hardly stopped also applies to advanced countries in Europe. Indeed, in most of these countries income growth has been more rapid for those in the middle and lower levels of the income distribution than it has been in the United States, even if, as in the United States, income growth has slowed from its pace before 1979.[45] Part of this has to do with the fact that the right has been considerably less successful in rolling back the European welfare states than commonly believed. These states, while under attack, have still managed to successfully supplement earnings growth with government transfer growth, producing relatively superior income gains for the middle class and poor. As sociologist Lane Kenworthy notes:

[T]here have been some cutbacks [to the European welfare states] but they've been mostly minor. And much of the cutting has consisted of rectifying earlier overshooting—the Dutch disability program of the 1970s, Sweden's sickness insurance, pensions in continental and southern Europe. So, for example, a country might reduce its replacement rate for unemployment insurance from 90% to 80%. . . . I think most who argue that there have been large cutbacks simply aren't familiar with the data.

Others [argue] that many western European countries have moved in the direction of encouraging or requiring employment. Does this count as a cutback? I say no. I think the sensible left . . . agrees that "the good society" isn't one in which adults are in paid work as little as possible. That was the dream in the 1970s, but no longer. So policies to facilitate, encourage, and in some instances, require employment are part of a "sideways" shift to a different welfare state, rather than a step backward.[46]

In other words, they are moving (albeit with many a bump along the road) toward the sort of opportunity state described in this book, rather than simply eliminating the welfare state.

Of course, as in the United States, the years since 1979 in Europe have also seen substantial progress on gender and sexual preference equality, on the environment, on life expectancy and on all the other various quality of life indicators mentioned above. Thus, as for the United States, it makes no sense to wallow in nostalgia for the Europe of yesterday and deny the real progress that has been made in the last 30–40 years.

HAS THE GREAT RECESSION RUINED EVERYTHING?

The final refuge for leftists who insist on pessimism is the economic and political havoc wrought by the Great Recession of 2008–09. That is, even if they (reluctantly) grant that some significant progress was made across advanced countries from the 1970s to 2007, the subsequent catastrophic meltdown of the financial system, adoption of budget austerity, extremely slow recovery and poor economic performance, and now the rise of right-wing populism that scapegoats immigrants, indicate a bleak future for the left and the middle and lower strata whose interests leftists seek to advance.

It indicates nothing of the sort. Start with the United States. It is true that recovery from the Great Recession has been quite slow compared to the typical recession (though it has been considerably faster than in most European countries). But it is also true that the Great Recession, as its name implies, was a particularly brutal recession and induced by a financial crisis to boot, two factors that have historically been barriers to a fast recovery. And it is certainly true that the pace of recovery has been significantly slowed by policy error (though not as much as in Europe), starting with a stimulus bill that was funded at inadequate levels, an error that was exacerbated by the turn to austerity in 2011 and the continued failure to mount a fiscal response to "secular stagnation." So there are reasons why the recovery has been slow that do not portend unending poor economic performance and the grinding down of the middle class. On the contrary, these reasons suggest that with the passage of time and correction of increasingly obvious policy errors, future economic performance is likely to be much better.

It is also important to focus on how much things have actually improved since the crisis, even if that improvement has been slow. The unemployment rate by summer of 2016 was running under 5 percent—close to full employment—down from its high of 10 percent in 2009, with wages finally starting to rise.[47] Household incomes by that time, according to CPS data analyzed by Sentier Research, had finally reached close to their pre-recession high.[48] In other words, while it has taken much longer than it should have, the economic situation is now much better than it was in the years immediately after the crisis, with considerable upside potential for the future.

This is real progress. Still, it cannot be denied that, if you combine pre-crisis and post-crisis periods together, the new century has, at least so far, been an era of exceptionally poor economic performance, especially in terms of income and wages. This makes the deep pessimism of some on the left understandable even if a poor fit for where we are now and where we are going. But it is less understandable how this pessimism has infected evaluations of the Obama administration and what it managed to accomplish.

THE VERY REAL ACCOMPLISHMENTS OF THE OBAMA ADMINISTRATION

A good example is Obama's first major accomplishment, the 2009 stimulus bill (aka the American Recovery and Reinvestment Act). Yes, the level of stimulus in the bill was too small (i.e., given the depth of the contraction, it should have been more like $1.3 trillion instead of $800 billion) and Obama may have made some mistakes in how it was negotiated.[49] But it was responsible for arresting the free-fall of the economy and preventing a very deep recession from becoming a full-scale depression. Studies indicate that unemployment and job loss, as bad as they were, would have been considerably worse had the bill not passed.[50]

Moreover, and critically, there is remarkably little appreciation of how much and how effectively the bill advanced a number of different priorities of the left. Start with clean energy. In 1999, President Clinton proposed a $6.3 billion clean energy bill that died a very quick legislative death. But the stimulus bill poured *$90 billion* into clean energy, more than 14 times what Clinton proposed!

The clean energy component of the stimulus bill did many things. As summarized by journalist Michael Grunwald, author of the definitive book on the stimulus, *The New New Deal*, it financed

> unprecedented government investments in a smarter grid, cleaner coal, energy efficiency in every imaginable form, "green-collar" job training, electric vehicles and the infrastructure to support them, advanced biofuels and the refineries to brew them, renewable power from the sun, the wind, and the heat below the earth, and factories to manufacture all that green stuff in the United States.[51]

In short, this was a massive government intervention into a critically important area that was (and is) a very high priority of the left. It was designed to jolt the flagging U.S. clean energy industry to life and double renewable power generation within Obama's first term—which it did. And it laid the basis for continuing advance in everything from battery storage to the energy grid to advanced research to factories and infrastructure.

But that's not all! The stimulus bill also invested $27 billion in computerizing the American medical records system, $8 billion in high-speed rail, $7 billion in expanding the country's high-speed internet network to underserved communities and on and on . . . not to mention "standard" stimulus measures like tax cuts and maintenance and upgrading of existing infrastructure. As noted by Grunwald, the bill "included America's biggest foray into industrial policy since FDR, the biggest expansion of anti-poverty initiatives since LBJ, the biggest middle-class tax cut since Ronald Reagan, and the biggest infusion of research money ever."[52]

Not too shabby. But of course the Obama administration's accomplishments hardly stop there. Above all, there is the Affordable Care Act (ACA), the radical transformation of the U.S. health care system into a near-universal system with a recognized government responsibility to ensure that citizens have access to health care—a goal the left has sought to attain for literally a hundred years going back to the Progressive Era. ACA works through a very complicated system of insurance subsidies for individuals, expansion of Medicaid, insurer regulations, cost containment measures, new taxes on the wealthy and government oversight.

It is true that the ACA-reformed system is far from ideal. It is also true that it is far better than what the United States had before and has worked remarkably well so far in terms of both extending health insurance coverage (20 million covered; uninsured rate down from 16 to 9 percent of the population) and containing health care costs.[53] It is far more likely now that the ACA will be built upon and improved, so that it extends coverage and reduces costs even more, than that it will be eliminated, as conservatives strenuously advocate. In this, it will be like the original gap-riddled Social Security program, which had to be modified repeatedly over time so that it came closer and closer to its goal of eliminating poverty among the elderly.

Another major Obama administration achievement is the Dodd-Frank Act, the first serious attempt to crack down on Wall Street in a generation. Besides creating government tools to single out and regulate "systematically important financial institutions" and even seize them in a crisis, the law has increased capital requirements for banks, restricted their ability to make speculative investments (the "Volcker rule"), successfully reduced financial sector leverage and established an important and vigorous new agency, the Consumer Financial Protection Bureau. These are significant reforms that have, in fact, made the financial system safer and less prone to crisis, even if there remains much that can and should be done.[54]

Obama is also responsible for a raft of other reforms, many of which would be signature achievements in another administration.[55] These include a transformative restructuring of the student loan program that ended private lender involvement, expanded Pell grants for low-income students by $36 billion and significantly eased student debt liabilities; loans and other assistance that saved the U.S. auto industry and pushed it onto its currently successful trajectory; the repeal of "don't ask, don't tell" in the military and crucial participation in the Supreme Court case that made same-sex marriage legal across the country; and bold executive actions on the environment to reduce U.S. greenhouse gas emissions in tandem with a new climate change agreement in Paris to reduce global emissions.

Put all this together and it is quite reasonable to characterize Obama's presidency as one of the most consequential of modern times—a presidency that has not just been good for progressive priorities, but *very* good, indeed, outstanding. As political scientist Paul Pierson has put it:

When you add the ACA to the reforms in the stimulus package, Dodd-Frank, and his various climate initiatives, I don't think there is any doubt: On domestic issues Obama is the most consequential and successful Democratic president since LBJ. It isn't close.[56]

Moreover, Hillary Clinton proposed to double down on Obama's progressive achievements while pursuing substantial new initiatives on other key progressive priorities. Among other commitments, she wanted to extend and strengthen the ACA, Dodd-Frank and Obama's clean energy initiatives; invest $275 billion in infrastructure and scientific research; establish universal pre-K; make community college free and further reduce student debt; guarantee paid family and medical leave; raise the minimum wage to $12/hour; and provide a pathway to citizenship for undocumented immigrants. Thus, the Obama administration not only accomplished an enormous amount of great importance to the left, but set the Democratic Party on a far more determined and aggressive course to pursuing progressive aims in the future.

So, where's the love? Why do so many on the U.S. left have such a pessimistic take on Obama and his many impressive accomplishments? A primary reason certainly is the unsatisfactory nature of the slow economic recovery, which seems to underscore the dominance of the very wealthy and the disjuncture between their economic health and the unmet needs in the rest of the population. This is an understandable sentiment and not without merit as an assessment of what needs to be fixed.

But it does not follow, of course, that the Obama administration made little progress in making the country better. In fact, the reverse is true; it made considerable progress in an unfavorable environment. So there is something else going on here that is short-circuiting positive sentiment on the left even where positive sentiment seems eminently deserved. This short-circuit can be located in a lack of understanding of what is and is not possible when growth is slow and economic outcomes are relatively poor for most people. Such an economic situation places intrinsic limits on the ability of the left to develop sustained support for expansive programs and successfully implement them. Thus, instead of blaming Obama for not doing more, the energies of the left could be more productively devoted to figuring out how to kindle faster and better-distributed economic growth. Then, much would be possible that currently isn't.

POOR ECONOMIC PERFORMANCE IS THE MAIN PROBLEM, BUT IT CAN BE SOLVED

One need look no further than the advanced countries of Europe to see just how badly a poor economic situation can hobble the left. As noted in chapter three, European countries, particularly those in the Eurozone, have suffered more economically than the United States because they have administered more austerity to their economies. And they have been much slower than the United States in discarding policies that have harmed their economies because of their limited room for fiscal maneuver, intrinsic in the structure of the EU and Eurozone, and severe pressure from the Troika economic authorities and from Germany to stay the course. As a result, growth has been painfully slow in most countries with continued high unemployment.

Naturally this situation has led to a great deal of resentment and economic discontent in these countries. But have these sentiments benefitted the left? By and large, no. In fact, these sentiments have bred fear and pessimism about change and suspicion of, not support for, government and government action. This has undercut the left, a situation that has been exacerbated by European social democrats' tendency to embrace Grand Coalitions between left and right simply to be in government. In so doing, they have tended to accept the current (unworkable) European fiscal framework, with attendant austerity measures and continued economic stagnation.

This situation reflects both the objective difficulties of the current economic situation and the relative weakness of today's labor and social democratic parties. These problems have led many social democrats to conclude they really have no choice but to enter Grand Coalitions and "make the best of a bad situation." The same logic has led many social democrats to accept the basic austerity framework but attempt to soften its effects. To do otherwise, their thinking has runs, would be irresponsible and unproductive.

However, the fact is that the current course is not working because it cannot work. There is no particularly good economic reason to think that continued austerity, even if softened by the presence of social democrats in government, and even if leavened with some much-needed reforms of the welfare state, will produce robust economic growth. Paul Krugman, Joseph Stiglitz, Amartya Sen, Dani

Rodrik, Simon Wren-Lewis and many other economists, including Thomas Piketty, have been making this case for years and, so far, their arguments line up very well with observed outcomes.

Nor is there any particularly good political reason to think that social democratic parties will benefit from their "responsible" administration of budget austerity, even if (or perhaps especially if) they are partnered with the right in doing so. Voters tend to punish parties that are perceived as hurting them and this tendency may be accentuated by the perceived contradiction between social democrats' current policies and historic commitments. Voters also tend to reward outsiders and populists in such situations and they have done so.

It is true that some of these electoral benefits have gone to parties to the left of the social democrats, the so-called left populist parties like Podemos (Spain), Syriza (Greece), Socialist Party (Netherlands), Five Star Movement (Italy) and Socialist People's Party (Denmark), so it's not the case that all segments of the left have suffered from this dynamic. However the chief beneficiaries of rising distaste for the economically depressed status quo, especially in northern Europe, have been right populist parties like the National Front (France), UKIP (Britain), Freedom Party (Austria), True Finns (Finland) and Party for Freedom (Netherlands). As political scientists Manuel Funke, Moritz Schularick and Christopher Trebesch have shown in an influential paper, "Going to Extremes: Politics after Financial

Crisis, 1870–2014," this is entirely consistent with the historic pattern in the aftermaths of large and lingering crises, where far-right populist parties driven heavily by xenophobia toward immigrants and minorities experience a surge in support.[57]

Of course, this is exactly what we have seen with the rise of European right populist parties that typically feature active hostility to immigrant populations combined with defending the welfare state for native residents. Their rise is as unsettling as it is predictable, given the prolonged economic difficulties.

That is true as well of the hemorrhaging of support for European social democrats. Overall, average support for these parties has fallen by about a third to lows not seen in 70 years and party after party has fallen to historic lows in their respective national elections.[58] Obviously, this has weakened the left overall, even if other segments of the left have achieved some gains. And the situation has not been helped by the general reluctance of social democratic parties to maximize left influence by uniting all left parties in coalition.

So is all lost in Europe? At least there, is not pessimism on the left fully justified? Not at all. Start with the fact that, despite relentless pressure in the current austerity climate, there has been only limited success in rolling back the basics of the European welfare states (though of course there has been considerable success in making people suffer needlessly). And the surging part of the European right, the populists, by and large, are defenders of the welfare state. They have no interest in seeing it dismantled.

Moreover, the current difficulties of the left in Europe have little to do with fundamental limits set on social advance by the depredations of capitalism, globalization or neoliberalism. Such pessimism is not justified, given that the real problem and its solution are simple and clear. If austerity can be dismantled and healthy growth resumed, there is, in fact, considerable room for further social advance down the road to vibrant opportunity states that preserve the best of current welfare states, while extending and modifying them for a new era.

The end of austerity and the resumption of growth are highly likely to happen eventually, though the road may be rough and twisting. There is simply no viable alternative to relaxing fiscal rules and moving the Eurozone and EU toward some sort of fiscal and democratic union so that this growth can take place. Francois Hollande of France tried to move in this direction but he blinked, as it were, in the face of German intransigence. Matteo Renzi of Italy also tried to break the logjam. He did not succeed but demand will continue to grow for change because national politicians cannot satisfy their constituents under the current regime. Once this demand reaches a critical level, a sufficiently powerful coalition of countries will form and change will happen.

Thus, despite the difficulties of the last 30 or 40 years, including the recent, particularly difficult post-crisis period, there is no reason for the left, either in the United States or Europe, to wallow in pessimism. Social and economic advances are still happening, new coalitions are still growing, and capitalism, with appropriate guidance from the left, is still capable of generating riches that can lift up everyone. In short, there is still everything to play for.

BUT ISN'T THE GAME RIGGED?

Some pessimistic leftists, however, may object that there is really nothing to play for because the game is rigged. That is, given the current influence of big money on politics, it is impossible to make any real progress until big money is dislodged from its current perch.

It is true that reducing the influence of money on politics would probably be of some help to the left and its aims. But a rigid insistence that this obstacle must be completely eliminated before further progress can be made is misguided. It betrays a lack of understanding of the obstacles to social change in a democratic capitalist society. In fact, much of the resistance to change comes from the public's changing and many-sided views about what it wants.

For example, as discussed earlier, the public in the United States tends to be operationally liberal but symbolically conservative. That is, the public generally wants the government to take action to remedy many social problems and provide many new services, but is suspicious of the government's ability to successfully pull off such initiatives.

Over time, as particular issues come to the fore, the left can make its case and convince the public that its operational liberalism should outweigh its symbolic conservatism on some initiatives, though of course the right and allied interests will continue to make the opposite case. This is a push-and-pull process, where the left will have some victories—particularly when economic growth is robust and well distributed—but many defeats as well.

This will be true even if big economic interests can't spend a nickel to support their favored candidates directly. In Maine and Arizona, "clean elections" systems have been established where campaigns are financed by a combination of very small donations and a lump sum from government. The result has been more contact between candidates and constituents and a somewhat wider pool of candidates but little change in the overall politics of these states in a left-right sense.[59] Even lobbying, the bête noire of many on the left, is most effective when an issue is not prominent and the mobilization of resources is concentrated on one side. When an issue rises in salience and both sides have significant resources committed, the effect of additional lobbying money on legislative success is small.

Thus, while the left should continue to press to limit the influence of money in politics, it is not true that current levels of money prohibit progressive advance or that reducing those levels would result in a tsunami of left advance. In the end the public will decide and it is to them the left must make its case.

ARE WE DOOMED BY GLOBAL WARMING?

Finally, the pièce de resistance of the pessimistic leftist is global warming—not that it exists and is a huge challenge (that is undeniable), but that the left is making no progress heading off a planet-devastating climate crisis. In fact, while many on the left sound notes of unremitting pessimism on this front, there has been dramatic progress on the availability and price of clean energy in recent years, which is likely the key to reducing greenhouse gas emissions to safe levels.

Consider the following. In the last few years, even as fossil fuel prices have declined, world investments in clean energy, chiefly wind and solar, have reached levels that are double those for fossil fuel.[60] Renewables now provide half of all new electric capacity.[61] And it is becoming increasingly common for clean energy in some areas to be cost-competitive with fossil fuels.

The rapidity with which clean energy is becoming cheaper and more available is stunning and still not widely appreciated. The cost of solar has fallen to 1/150th of its 1970s level and the amount of installed solar capacity has increased a staggering 115,000 times.[62] These exponential trends are hard to properly assess, even for those whose business it is to do so. For example, Ramez Naam, a proponent of clean energy, back in 2011 posited that solar power was following a kind of Moore's Law for energy (Moore's Law projected that microchips would double in efficiency every two years). Such efficiency gains would allow solar energy systems, which had by then fallen to about $3 a watt, to drop to only 50 cents a watt by 2030. However, Naam noted in the spring of 2015 that he had been way too conservative: solar power systems by early 2015 had already hit the 50 cent mark.[63]

Wind power, which tends to be complementary to solar power (the former best at night, the latter during the day), has been following a similar, if less steep trajectory. And, critically, energy storage, which is absolutely essential for these more intermittent sources of energy, is also rapidly dropping in price and increasing in efficiency.[64] The price per watt of lithium-ion battery storage of electricity dropped by about 90 percent between 1991 and 2005 and has continued to drop faster than projections since then. The price and efficiency improvement rates for battery storage have actually been faster than the corresponding (already high) rates for wind and solar over the same periods. And new battery technologies now in development could even accelerate price/efficiency gains, especially for grid energy storage.

These developments suggest that clean energy is well on its way to becoming cost-competitive with fossil fuels and, eventually, cost-advantaged (that is, cheaper). Thus, contrary to the green left pessimists, it is not the case that the green revolution can only succeed through immediate, drastic, coordinated taxation and regulation of fossil fuels all over the world—something that would be hugely difficult to pull off politically and especially unpopular in developing countries that need cheap energy to drive economic growth and pull their populations out of poverty. In fact, the green revolution is already making very significant progress, despite political obstacles.

And the green revolution will make even more progress as governments step up their efforts to promote clean energy. Governments, not just in the United States and Europe but in critical developing countries like China, have invested substantially in clean energy R&D, provided tax incentives and loans for start-up firms and promulgated regulations that promote clean energy usage. These efforts to tilt the playing field will only become more prominent in the future, as declining prices make renewable energy an easier sell and the economic benefits of investing in the clean energy transition become ever more obvious.

It is also likely that international agreements like the 2015 Paris agreement will make a significant contribution to the eventual triumph of green energy and prevention of a possible climate crisis. The Paris agreement has been criticized by some on the green left for lacking sufficient scope and enforcement mechanisms to solve the global warming problem. But that misses the point of the agreement, which was not to "solve" the problem but rather to start a process. And it greatly underestimates the significance of getting all countries to sign onto addressing the problem, set concrete goals on emissions reductions and agree to come together every five years to assess progress and set new goals. This framework will allow countries to interact with one another in an organized and ongoing way to combat climate change, rather than fight about fanciful goals that are not cognizant of economic and political realities and therefore are highly unlikely to be effective.

Even fracking, anathema to many on the U.S. left, should properly be viewed as progress in the current context.[65] The most important fact to keep in mind here is that producing electricity with natural gas produces only about half the carbon dioxide emissions as using coal. Thus, since drastic price decreases for natural gas generated by the success of fracking have allowed natural gas to make considerable progress in replacing coal as an energy source, the effect on U.S. emissions has been net positive. Indeed, U.S. carbon dioxide emissions have actually gone down since their 2007 peak, rather than up as they were expected to do, and fracking is partly (though not solely) responsible for this.

Of course, both coal and natural gas produce far more emissions than renewables, which are essentially emissions free. It would be nice if we could just wave a magic wand and replace all fossil fuels today, including natural gas, with clean energy sources. But we cannot do that and therefore a transition strategy is needed while fossil fuel usage is still a big part of the economy; fracking and natural gas are part of that strategy. Meanwhile, efforts to tilt the playing field toward renewables will continue and the price of clean energy will continue to drop rapidly. In the end, natural gas will go the way of other fossil fuels, but today it is playing a valuable role in accelerating the move away from coal, by far the worst polluting of these fuels.

The other main objection to fracking, besides the fact that it produces a fossil fuel and is therefore bad, is that it commonly leads to negative effects, like polluted drinking water and earthquakes, in local communities. However, these effects are exaggerated; a 2015 EPA study found no systematic effect of fracking on local communities' drinking water (though some incidents have occurred).[66] Similarly, the National Academy of Sciences finds that fracking and related activities generally do not cause serious earthquake activity and the possibility of large seismic events can be avoided through appropriate precautions.[67] This is not to say fracking entails no risks—any large-scale industrial activity involves some risks. But those posed by fracking are of the sort that are amenable to better and more uniform regulation of the industry, particularly at the federal level. Banning fracking outright, as many on the left advocate, is not justified by the level of risk and, as we have seen, is actually counter-productive from an emissions-control perspective.

Overall, then, the common green left view that we are not making progress in the struggle to contain global warming is way too pessimistic. It is a classic example of letting the best be the enemy of the good, an all-too-common error in left analysis. In fact, serious progress is being made and trends are in place that hold great promise for solving the climate problem. It is—or should be—the job of the left to celebrate and accelerate these trends, not pooh-pooh them.

NO, PESSIMISM IS NOT A CHANGE MOTIVATOR

One final objection of the pessimists should be addressed. The more empirically oriented among them might grant that many of the positive trends identified in this chapter are real. However, they feel existing negative trends are real as well and it is the job of the left to highlight them, regardless of the net between positive and negative, since that is where the motivation for change will come from.

But this confuses the motivations of left activists with the motivations of average citizens. It is absolutely true that most left activists are fundamentally motivated by what they see as wrong and unjust in contemporary social arrangements. Their strong sense of what is wrong is what propels them into activity and allows them to sustain political commitment over long periods.

This is not, however, the way most people work. In the United States, for example, Americans generally adopt a bifurcated view of their situation that does not comport well with the relentless pessimism of many leftists. On the one hand, most Americans do tend to believe that many things have changed for the worse—that the economy has been doing poorly, that long-term trends have hurt security for average families, that leaders just don't get it. On the other hand, these very same Americans believe that *they* are holding up their end of the economic bargain, that *they* are working hard and doing right by their families, that *their* story is one of optimism and hope, not pessimism and despair. Even today, with most Americans embracing a negative economic story overall, many still believe a positive economic story applies to themselves (in a January, 2016 poll, 63 percent of the public, despite widespread discontent with the economic and political situation, still described themselves as "living the American Dream"[68]). Thus left pessimism appeals to only one side of Americans' outlook and completely misses the other.

Indeed, at times some on the left seem to revise the old forties' song to "accentuate the negative, ignore the positive and don't mess with Mr. In-between." The optimistic leftist rejects this approach, recognizing that pessimism promotes demobilization, while a sense that positive change has been, is and will continue to be possible makes it far easier to mobilize ordinary citizens for a better future. The next chapter sketches the contours of that brighter future—the left's twenty-first century.

FIVE

The Left's 21st Century

The first thing to note about the left's twenty-first century is that living standards should rise very substantially and that is a very good thing. Indeed, the left will play a central role in pushing that trend forward by saving capitalism from its tendencies toward stagnation, periodic crises and inequality—capitalism's "Piketty problem." The right has little interest in doing so; only the left has the proper incentive structure, emerging coalition and ideological commitments to guide capitalism onto a new and healthier growth path that can better support rising living standards.

This will take some time; cautious politicians and vested interests will resist change. But the political and economic imperatives of building the opportunity state are clear and will become more so over time, as the postindustrial progressive coalition continues to grow and the demand for better economic performance becomes ever stronger. This demand for better performance will eventually be met, even if gradually, with some setbacks along the way. And as living standards get on a healthier trajectory, much of the left agenda that seems difficult to push today will become much easier to sell to voters. As a result, the opportunity state will be strengthened.

A RICHER WORLD

How much are living standards likely to rise? Far more than people currently think. Consider the developing world first. As globalization and economic development proceed in these countries, we will more and more see not just the decline and possible elimination of extreme poverty, but the rise of large swathes of the developing world to the living standards currently enjoyed by the middle classes of the advanced world. Indeed, conventional projections indicate that world GDP per capita, currently only about one-quarter of today's U.S. level, should be nearly 50 percent higher than the current U.S. level by the end of this century.[1]

Projections for individual countries highlight the sweeping nature of likely economic changes in this century: Turkey, Mexico, Brazil, India, Indonesia and South Africa by 2100 should have GDP per capita levels from 70 percent higher than the current level in the United States to more than double that level. China is projected to have a GDP per capita level around two and a half times today's U.S. level. And a long list of countries should have per capita incomes in 2100 from 35 to 65 percent higher than the current U.S. level: Nigeria, Pakistan, Philippines, Cameroon, Senegal, Tanzania, Bangladesh, Vietnam, Cambodia, Honduras, El Salvador, Guatemala, Costa Rica and many others. Another long list of countries is expected to best the current U.S. per capita income level by amounts from 5 to 35 percent by 2100; only a handful of countries, like Zimbabwe, Eritrea and Burundi, are projected to still be below this level by 2100.

In short, the world and most people in it should be *much* richer by the year 2100. That means hundreds of millions— billions—of people attaining a standard of living that would be characterized as middle class in today's advanced countries. The left should see this development as very good news indeed. Many, many more people across the world will be able to lead lives largely free of material suffering, with comfort levels most global citizens can only dream about today. That should be applauded vigorously.

And material advance across the world will create much more favorable conditions for the left's key priorities: the extension and consolidation of democracy; the spread of modern, egalitarian norms on race, gender and sexuality; and, of course, robust mixed economies—opportunity states—that can combine the support citizens need to get ahead (education, health care, child care, social insurance) with the judicious regulation and state investments in infrastructure and science needed to ensure strong growth. Across the world, all these priorities will become much easier to meet as many more countries become rich by today's standards.

Turning to the advanced world, as noted earlier GDP per capita growth in the United States has been quite slow in the first part of the twenty-first century (only 0.9 percent per year) and household/family income growth even slower. But better days are coming, partly because of delayed recovery from the Great Financial Crisis, partly because of ongoing technological advance and partly because of better policies that will increasingly be adopted to mitigate inequality and promote faster growth.

Even if future per capita income growth fails to match the pace of the late twentieth century (which was itself slow by the standards of the immediate post–World War II period), the United States should be a far richer country by midcentury. Thomas Piketty projects that per capita income growth will slow to about 1.2 percent per year.[2] Organization of Economic Cooperation and Development (OECD) projections are somewhat more optimistic at 1.5 percent per year.[3] Both, however, are significantly lower than the 1.7 percent per year since 1973 and, especially, the 2.4 percent per year from 1946 to 1973.

But even under these projections, which reflect slow growth by historical standards, the United States will become much, much richer by 2050. At 1.2 percent per year, per capita income will be 50 percent higher than it is today; at 1.5 percent per year it will be 66 percent higher. And if the United States can be returned to its long-term post-1870 growth trajectory, 1.9 percent per year (still significantly lower than the postwar years), per capita income will be 90 percent higher at midcentury than today.

A much richer country should mean much richer people, especially if growth is reasonably well distributed, as will increasingly be the political and economic imperative going forward. How much richer? Today, median family income is about $70,000 (2014 dollars); at a 1.2 percent growth rate, it would rise to $105,000 by midcentury. Median household income, which includes single-person households, is lower—about $57,000 today—but would still rise to $86,000 by 2050 at this growth rate.[4]

At a 1.5 percent growth rate, the corresponding figures for median family and household income would be $116,000 and $94,000 by midcentury. And at the historic 1.9 percent per year growth rate, the corresponding median incomes would be $133,000 and $108,000.

A MASS UPPER MIDDLE CLASS

Of course, families and households vary considerably by size, so the same income can mean very different living standards when that income supports a single person or an entire family of four or five. Thus, to clarify the effect of these trends on living standards, it is useful to look at a standard household size and adjust household incomes to fit that standard size. Using a three-person household as the standard, economist Stephen Rose has shown that the median adult in the United States today enjoys a standard of living equivalent to $65,000 for a family of three.[5]

Using the same standard, Rose defines the upper middle class as those adults whose household incomes are the equivalent of $100,000 a year for a family of three, but less than $350,000. By this measure, over a quarter (29 percent) of U.S. adults are in the upper middle class today.[6] Interestingly, this analysis indicates that the biggest change since 1979 in class positions defined by these standardized income levels has been a dramatic rise in the size of the upper middle class, which more than doubled, from 13 to 29 percent of adults. The rich ($350,000+) have, as popular perception suggests, also increased, but they are still a very small group, only 1.8 percent of adults.

Also consistent with popular perception, the middle middle class ($50,000–$100,000 in adjusted income) has declined over this time period (down 7 points to 32 percent of adults). But it is also the case that the lower middle class ($30,000-$50,000 in income) has declined (down 7 points to 17 percent), as has the poor/near poor (less than $30,000, down 4 points to 20 percent). Thus, the rise of the upper middle class deserves a place of greater significance in the left's calculations going forward since this group appears to be absorbing the much-publicized declines in middling income groups.

Applying the previous growth rates to these data, the median adult by midcentury would have an adjusted income of $98,000 at 1.2 percent growth, $108,000 at 1.5 percent growth and $124,000 at 1.9 percent growth. That means that around half or more of the country by that time would enjoy the living standards of today's upper middle class (or even better).

Thus, a reasonable aspiration for the left in advanced countries should be to make current upper-middle-class affluence a majority lifestyle in coming decades and to raise the rest of the population as close to that level as possible. And in the developing world, the goal should be to raise a majority of these countries' populations to the current living standards of the advanced countries' middle middle and lower middle classes.

These goals may seem far-fetched, but they are attainable given decent, long-term economic growth and a reasonably fair distribution of the benefits from growth. The left should accept nothing less and, as noted, given the intimate connection in today's world between fair distribution and growth potential, the left is well positioned to be the leader in growth promotion. Indeed, it is really only the left that is well positioned to provide that leadership; the right is infatuated with supply-side and austerity doctrines that are fundamentally counter-productive and anti-growth. And of course the right doesn't take inequality seriously at all, failing especially to see its currently deleterious influence on economic performance.

TWENTY-FIRST-CENTURY OPPORTUNITY STATES

Decent growth and rising living standards, highly desirable in and of themselves, will underpin a whole host of other gains that accord with left priorities. This is because a richer society in which the typical citizen is experiencing a significant elevation of their living standards is a society much more open to investing in collective goods and helping all citizens prosper.

Consider the role of education. The role of education in promoting upward mobility is well established but so too is its role in promoting growth and mitigating inequality.[7] Perhaps no single area will be as central to twenty-first-century opportunity states as this one.

Therefore we will likely see massive investment in expanding access to education and improving its quality. This will certainly include the provision of universal pre-school, an intervention whose effectiveness is clear, with strong connections to better educational outcomes, particularly for poorer children. And we will certainly see a very substantial increase in access to a college education. This will include not only a substantially larger share of young people completing a four-year college degree but, critically, the development of a new "standard" level of education beyond the high school diploma. That will be a community college degree or equivalent—in other words, 14 years of education will replace the current 12 as the standard credential needed to satisfy minimal job requirements.

To facilitate this transition, we are likely to see, as Hillary Clinton advocated, attendance at community college made essentially free to all qualified applicants. This makes sense; if a community college degree becomes the new high school diploma, then community college, just like high school today, should be made publicly available at no cost. In addition, though it may take longer, we are likely to see, as Bernie Sanders advocated, free tuition at public four-year colleges and universities so that more of those wishing to bolster their credentials beyond 14 years of school can do so.

Other aspects of the opportunity state will see considerable expansion as society becomes richer. This will include provision of supplementary retirement accounts with universal enrollment, expansion of Social Security and Obamacare, paid family and medical leave, guaranteed access to affordable child care, and expanded income, training and public job provision supports for employment. As Lane Kenworthy notes, all of these programs can be seen as forms of public insurance.[8] It is risk management to protect vulnerable citizens who might otherwise not have access to (or lose through misfortune) adequate retirement or employment income, health care or child care. These are all crucial components to a successful modern life, and creating a safety net with public programs helps ensure that everyone has the opportunity to advance.

As such, these programs will be critical aspects of the twenty-first-century opportunity state. They will support everyone, but will be particularly important for poorer members of society, who are more likely to need this insurance and, without it, more likely to have their upward mobility stymied. A richer society with healthy growth is both more able to afford this expansion of opportunity and more likely to feel okay about doing so.

Investment in public goods will also be central to the left's twenty-first century. Indeed, the kind of economic growth advanced societies need and that will enable the achievement of the left's goals will not be possible without a substantial increase in such investment. At the current time, the rate of infrastructure investment in the United States is lower than it has been at any time since 1947.[9] This increased investment will take a number of forms.

Most obviously, there will be a ratcheting up of investment in basic physical infrastructure—airports, bridges, highways, school buildings, water, sewage and so on. In the United States, there is an enormous amount of repair and maintenance of existing infrastructure that is needed simply to remedy current deterioration and avoid further decline. The American Society of Civil Engineers estimates the needed expenditures here at around $3.6 trillion.[10]

Then, of course, one does not simply want to avoid decline but to actively invest for a more productive future.

Beyond investing in new infrastructure in traditional areas (for example, high-speed trains), this will entail massive efforts to expand and improve current digital and clean energy infrastructure, which is woefully short of future "new economy" needs.

Linked to these efforts, there will be considerable expansion of investment in research and development, especially in the clean energy area. As noted earlier, both the science and the infrastructure that led to the IT revolution owe an enormous amount to government support and investment. The same will be true, except perhaps more so, for the impending clean energy revolution.

The clean energy revolution will have many components, and certainly one of them is seeking to level the playing field between clean and dirty energy through tax and regulatory changes. But it will require much more than that because, in the end, the key to the clean energy revolution will be cheap and reliable clean energy that is truly cost-competitive with fossil fuels. That in turn will necessitate technological breakthroughs that join truly inexpensive clean energy to efficient storage and integration with the power grid. Government investment, both directly and through public-private partnerships, is the key to promoting rapid breakthroughs and providing the support and infrastructure to take them to scale.

The first boom in clean energy innovation in the 1970s was driven by a quadrupling of government investment in response to that decade's oil price shocks.[11] The second wave in the 2000s was turbocharged by the massive clean energy investments of the 2009 stimulus bill (detailed in chapter four). However, in both cases, a high level of government involvement was not sustained and innovation slowed. Most recently, even though clean energy prices continue to fall, the clean energy portfolios of venture capital firms have declined by 75 percent as stimulus support for clean energy R&D, infrastructure, demonstration projects and start-ups has dried up.

This is the wrong direction if we want to accelerate the transition away from fossil fuels. Today, the federal budget for clean energy R&D is only about $6.4 billion, considerably lagging federal research budgets for space exploration ($13 billion), medicine ($31 billion) and defense ($78 billion). The 20-country Mission Innovation agreement announced by Obama calls for doubling clean energy R&D budgets by 2020. Given the importance of this vital area and the central role of public investment in future growth, this will likely be just a down payment on the level ultimately committed by government to the clean energy revolution.

The case for these public investments could not be clearer; decades hence people will look back and wonder why these investments were downplayed for so long. They have played, and will play in the future, a central role in raising productivity, promoting strong growth, maintaining full employment and facilitating transitions from one economic era to another. There is perhaps no other area where government expenditures have such a high payoff and, indeed, typically pay for themselves over the long haul. That is, rather than adding to the national debt burden over time, they reduce it because of the extra revenue generated from a stronger economy. This is why so many economists today are practically screaming for more of these investments and wringing their hands about our slowness in doing so.

The case is so overwhelming that it will eventually carry the day. There is simply no other way advanced societies can get from where they are today to where they want and need to be. Even conservatives will be carried along by this tide as they seek to remain relevant on the issue of growth. They will, of course, disagree with the left on the exact nature of these investments and their size, but it will no longer be viable to cling to the quasi-libertarian stance that the market will solve all and the economy has no need for government involvement.

This will be true both in the United States and in Europe, despite the obstacles presented in Europe by Eurozone and EU rules and governing structures. The manifest failure of austerity economics to produce strong growth, combined with its political unpopularity, will eventually lead to its demise, along with a rewriting of the European rules and structures currently producing dysfunctional outcomes.[12] Then it will be possible for European countries to pursue expansionary policies focused on public investment, growth and employment while making reasonable reforms to welfare state programs, probably along the "flexicurity" lines pioneered by the Nordic countries.

Indeed, a solid growth trajectory driven by public investment will be the key to reforming European welfare states and turning them into twenty-first-century opportunity states. European publics will be far more open to change once growth has returned and living standards have risen; lacking such growth the continual clamoring by elites for "structural reform" is as counter-productive as the austerity economics to which it is typically linked.

The rise of the opportunity state will mean not only more growth but also less inequality. The most common position on inequality today is that it will continue to go up. But this is just as ill-founded a view as the original Kuznets position that inequality will continue to go down once advanced societies pass a certain economic level. A better concept is that societies go through what economist Branko Milanovic calls "Kuznets cycles"—long periods in which a constellation of forces push inequality up, eventually to unsustainable levels, followed by long corrective periods in which inequality is pushed down. And then inequality goes back up again, starting another cycle.[13]

We are now near the top of the Kuznets cycle that began in the 1970s. Inequality may continue rising for a while but, as advanced societies start moving along the growth-oriented opportunity state path, inequality will begin coming down. The reduction in inequality will itself be helpful to growth, promoting a virtuous feedback loop between lower inequality, growth and the continuing advance of the opportunity state.

DEMOCRACY, PEACE AND SOCIAL EQUALITY

Some of the left's most cherished goals have to do with democracy, tolerance and social equality. It is highly likely that progress toward these goals will continue throughout the twenty-first century.

Start with democracy. The rapid spread of democracy around the world was mentioned earlier. There were very few democracies in the years after World War II but today a solid majority (56 percent) of countries can fairly be characterized as democracies.[14] That's remarkable progress.

We should expect this progress to continue as the world becomes richer. Economic growth, particularly to the extent it enables larger middle classes and higher education levels, leads to demand for democratic norms and practices where they do not exist. Over the long term, these demands will be met and the twenty-first century will likely witness a near-universalization of basic democracy—free and fair competitive elections with universal suffrage and basic freedoms of press, association and speech—as a regime standard in all parts of the world.

The spread of democracy in the context of rising affluence should lead to a host of other good things that are on the left's agenda. We should see a very substantial increase in the support for, and practice of, equality by gender, race and sexual orientation in countries around the world. Of course, many countries still have far to go in these areas but democracy will facilitate progress as new, more educated and liberal younger generations replace older, conservative ones.

Higher levels of democracy should also lead to less violence. Though not widely appreciated, the world today is a considerably less violent place than it ever has been. As psychologist Steven Pinker notes, "The worldwide rate of death from interstate and civil war combined has juddered downward . . . from almost 300 per 100,000 world population during World War II, to almost 30 during the Korean War, to the low teens during the era of the Vietnam War, to single digits in the 1970s and 1980s, to less than 1 in the twenty-first century."[15]

One of the biggest reasons for this stunning decline in state/civil war violence is the rise of democracy. Democracies are far less likely to go to war with one another than non-democracies are. Therefore, as democracy has become more common, we have fewer war-related deaths. As the twenty-first century unfolds, the continued rise of democracy should reinforce the trend toward peaceful resolution of disputes.

BUT WHAT ABOUT ISIS? WHAT ABOUT CHINA?

The ongoing threat of terrorism does not negate this ongoing trend. No one can be happy, for example, about the rise of ISIS (aka the Islamic State). But it is important to keep this development in global perspective. There are perhaps 30,000 fighters affiliated with ISIS. This is 30,000 more than is desirable, but that compares to 1.6 billion Muslims world-wide or, if you like, about 200 million in Indonesia alone, where ISIS or ISIS-like formations have no presence.

There is nothing intrinsic in Islam that makes it incompatible with modernization and social progress, any more than Christianity, despite its lengthy association with feudalism, autocracy, war and torture, has proved incompatible with such advance. The overwhelming majority of Muslims want modern economic development, more education, upward mobility and the material benefits of a Western middle-class lifestyle. And they tend to have a very unfavorable view of ISIS and Al Qaeda and reject their methods.[16]

Given that ISIS does not promise and certainly cannot provide any of these improvements (witness their disastrous administration of the areas they have controlled), their long-term appeal to the populations of Muslim countries should be very limited. And as these countries continue along their development paths, with more educated and affluent populations, they will instead become more fertile grounds for democracy, social equality and other priorities of the left. This may take some time and there will be setbacks—witness the aftermath of the "Arab Spring"—but it is a far better bet than the idea that Islamic countries are doomed to religious authoritarianism and dominance by extremists.

Nor is it likely that ISIS and ISIS-like groups can dramatically interfere with the welfare and progress of advanced countries. Terrorist incidents are tragedies and it seems plausible that we will see more of them in Europe and America in the future no matter how much intelligence and security efforts improve. But ISIS and its ilk are simply not powerful enough to do more than launch isolated attacks that generate fear. They will not fundamentally threaten societal stability in these countries.

While ISIS is not and will not become powerful enough to be a real threat to the West, the view that China could be such a threat is more plausible. It is the largest country by population in the world and, as measured by the IMF on a Purchasing Power Parity (PPP) basis, now has the biggest economy (though still far behind the United States and other countries on a per capita basis).

It is also a country still ruled by a Communist Party and lacking true democratic norms and freedoms. As China's influence and power continue to grow, some worry that its authoritarian government will undermine the international system and set back progress toward democracy and human rights. Besides assuming that China has an incentive to disrupt the international system (it doesn't), this view assumes, also incorrectly, that Chinese authoritarianism will not itself change much in the future. On the contrary, China has already changed a great deal in recent decades, with far more freedom of expression and rule of law as the country has developed economically.

This progress is likely to continue as China becomes richer, the middle class continues to grow and workers press demands for better treatment and higher wages. The

Communist Party will eventually be forced to adapt to the preferences of its changing population, institutionalizing some democratic forms and enhancing China's woefully inadequate social welfare system. This will not make China into a Western-style democracy anytime soon but it will have more and more in common with this model as its economic and social progress continues. Thus, the direction of change in China should cut for the priorities of the left, not against them as many fear.

RIGHT POPULISM: THIS TOO SHALL PASS

Nothing terrifies the left—and many on the right as well—more than the upsurge of right populism in advanced countries. The rise of Donald Trump in the United States and his unexpected capture of the presidency provides the most recent illustration of this trend but many European countries have also seen right populist parties gain in strength in recent years. The fear is that right populists will ride a tide of economic anxiety and cultural resentment to a commanding political position, displacing the traditional center-right and providing a permanent barrier to left advance—perhaps even threatening democracy itself.

This fear is overblown for several reasons. The first is that the right populist movement is riding on demographic borrowed time. Typically, the greatest strength of these parties comes from the votes of less-educated aging whites. But to a greater or lesser degree, the population weight of these voters is declining across countries. In the United States, the white non-college-educated share of voters declined by 19 percentage points just between the 1988 and 2012 presidential elections. Projections indicate that this group's share of voters should continue to decline by 2–3 points every presidential election for decades.[17]

The flip side is that the left's burgeoning postindustrial coalition is composed of groups for whom right populist cultural attitudes are anathema. As these groups continue to grow, their values too will be in the ascendancy, crowding out the space for right populism. This is not to say that right populism will not continue to be a problem for some time but rather that over the medium to long term the movement has intrinsically limited growth potential.

The second reason why right populism will not grow as much as people fear is that the movement is dependent on relatively bad economic times. Once good times return, economies are on solid growth paths and the benefits of growth are reasonably well diffused—as this book argues is likely to happen—populist anger and nativist sentiment will abate, undercutting these parties' electoral appeal.

That does not mean these parties will suddenly vanish; some disaffected, mostly older voters will remain attached. But without the juice provided by economic stagnation, the argument that immigrants cause all problems and that the overall system is completely corrupt will become less compelling and yield fewer electoral dividends.

Finally, the political dynamic unleashed by right populism will actually contribute to its own demise. Right populism is distinguished by not only its nativist cultural attitudes but also by its economic populism and rejection of austerity economics. The National Front in France, for example, has become steadily more militant in its defense of social programs and resistance to spending cuts as it has become more popular. Other European right populist parties have followed a similar course. And in the United States, Donald Trump's successful capture of the Republican presidential nomination was importantly driven by his rejection of standard Republican talking points on cutting government spending—especially on programs like Medicare and Social Security—and his advocacy of large spending increases on infrastructure.

The competition this is creating for voters on the right will force more mainstream conservatives to back off their commitment to austerity economics and rediscover the virtues of some government programs and spending. And even on the left, the rise of right populism will undercut the political rationale for the "responsible" soft austerity that has inveigled so many European social democrats and that still has a presence within the American Democratic Party. When so many voters on the right are rejecting the need to cut government, it makes no political sense to stick with austerity as an economic program on the grounds that opposing it isolates the left. On the contrary, it is supporting austerity and failing to deliver growth that isolates the left. The left will eventually take this lesson to heart.

Thus, the rise of right populism will ultimately lead across the political spectrum to a more favorable environment for growth-oriented opportunity-state policy approaches. These approaches will lead to better, and better-distributed, economic performance, which in turn will undermine the appeal of right populism. In the end, the right populism of the 2010s will likely have no more staying power than the agrarian populism of the 1880s and 1890s, which was similarly based on declining demographics and similarly undercut by the transition to a new economic system.

HUMAN NATURE AND THE OPPORTUNITY STATE

Perhaps the most fundamental objection to this optimistic view of the twenty-first century and the projected role of the opportunity state is that it runs contrary to human nature. That is, it presupposes more generous and group-oriented behavior by human beings in the aggregate than they are really capable of. Actually, the contrary is true; the opportunity state is far more consistent with our evolving understanding of human nature than the conservative alternatives, which tend to assume that human nature is fundamentally selfish and disconnected from the common good.

That view and its still considerable influence can be traced back to the 1957 publication of Ayn Rand's *Atlas Shrugged*, a 1,200-page novel that, in essence, advocated the unfettered pursuit of self-interest as the organizing principle for society.[18] Despite the fact that the book became a best-seller, not many critics and intellectuals took it or its thesis seriously at the time. Who could possibly believe that a society based strictly on selfishness could work?

Despite skepticism, the theory of selfishness continued to gain traction over the next several decades. One of the key supports for the theory came from evolutionary biologist Richard Dawkins. His 1976 book, *The Selfish Gene*, argued that the "selfish" gene is the fundamental unit of natural selection and has only one imperative: to successfully reproduce itself in competition with other genes.[19] Humans (and other animals), as bearers of these "selfish" genes, will therefore carry those traits—and only those traits—that help the genes reproduce. Dawkins implied that was all you needed to know to understand human nature, and his book quickly led to an explosion of "selfish gene"–based explanations for every aspect of human behavior.

Then, in 1980, Milton Friedman, with his wife, Rose, published *Free to Choose*, a no-holds-barred polemic in favor of self-interested individuals making "rational," unregulated decisions.[20] The Friedmans argued against anything that interfered with this process, especially government action. So, in a powerful conjunction of economics and evolutionary biology, Ayn Rand's glorification of selfishness gained the imprimatur of serious science. Being selfish was just human nature and should not be fought. Indeed, any attempt to do so was bound to do more harm than good. Thus was the original reaction to *Atlas Shrugged* turned on its head. Who could possibly believe that a society based on anything other than selfishness could work?

No doubt Ayn Rand would have been delighted with the progress of her big idea in the subsequent decade. Ronald Reagan was elected U.S. president and Margaret Thatcher became prime minister of the UK, both practicing a politics best summarized as "government is the problem, not the solution," and both preaching an economic gospel that glorified the individual pursuit of wealth above all else. And Rand's disciple, Alan Greenspan, was appointed head of the Federal Reserve in 1987 and remained there for 19 years, treated reverentially by both Democratic and Republican administrations.

Also in the 1980s, the breakdown of the postwar welfare states became undeniable and, by, the end of the decade, the Soviet Union and other "socialist" countries had ignominiously collapsed. Conservatives argued that all this was real-world confirmation of Rand's core idea: those who interfered with human selfishness would reap the whirlwind.

But right at its moment of greatest success, the conservative case on human nature was being fatally undermined. New thinking and research in evolutionary science showed that the "selfishness is all" camp was completely missing the mark on what makes humanity distinctive.[21] It is not competition for individual reproductive success but rather *cooperation* for group reproductive success, facilitated by our capacities for symbolic thought (language) and transmission of learned information (culture), that has led to our success as a species.

In short, the key to understanding human nature is not the selfish gene, but rather the "selfless gene." The selfless gene allowed our ancestors to think and act as a group, thereby outcompeting other chimp-like species—literally leaving them in the dust. Moreover, our cooperative nature allowed us to build ever more complex ways of interacting with one another, which led to further evolution in the traits that facilitate cooperation (referred to as "gene-culture coevolution"). The end result of this dynamic was civilization and, eventually, the global interconnected society we live in today.

This is who we are. We are defined by our sense of fairness, adherence to group norms, willingness to punish those who violate such norms, willingness to share, and willingness to work for the good of the group, along with the high-level cognitive and cultural traits that enable us to be that way. We are not a species of seven billion selfish individuals, interested in only our own welfare and willing to cheerfully break any rule and hurt any other individual to secure it. Indeed, we think of such people as sociopaths, and if their tendencies actually dominated humanity, we would still be back on the savannah with the rest of the chimp-like species.

So the conservative view on human nature is just plain

wrong. It's just not the case that societies must rely exclusively on self-interest or die. In fact, they can only live and prosper by transcending self-interest and harnessing the group-oriented instincts that make us human. This finding has enormous significance, not least for economic theory.

This is because the standard model of economics is based around precisely the assumption that people are solely motivated by self-interested concerns. As we have just seen, they aren't, which poses a rather fundamental problem for mainstream economics. The problem deepens when the other key part of the standard economic model is recalled: that a person rationally, efficiently and effectively pursues that self-interest at all times, carefully calculating probabilities and assessing costs and benefits so they can get the best possible deal for themselves—like a sort of self-interested Mr. Spock. People aren't like that, either.

The evidence blasting apart the standard economic model has been accumulating for quite some time as the fields of experimental and behavioral economics have expanded. Instead of assuming that the discipline's very conservative core assumptions are true and proceeding from there, these branches of economics actually test the assumptions. The following examples are two simulations, or games, that behavioral scientists ran to study how selfish (or not) people are.[22]

In the "dictator game," there are two players: a "proposer" and a second player. The proposer is given a sum of money and asked to give some amount to the second player. The proposer is told she will be allowed to keep the rest and there will be no second round. A truly rational decision maker would give the second player nothing and keep the full amount for herself. But in actual experimental situations, a majority of proposers gave away amounts ranging from 20 to 60 percent of the whole.

In the "ultimatum game," there is a responder and a proposer. Again, the proposer is given a certain amount of money. The proposer is told that they can offer some portion of that money to the responder, who may accept or reject the offer. If the responder accepts, the players both get to keep the agreed-upon money. If the responder rejects the offer, neither player gets anything.

The truly rational proposer would offer the least possible amount—say, a dollar—and the truly rational responder would accept the offer, since she would realize that otherwise she would get nothing. But that's not what happened. In experiments conducted around the world, the vast majority of proposers offered between 40 and 60 percent of the total amount. More surprisingly, offers below 30 percent were routinely rejected by responders—both players making choices at odds with their own self-interest.

There are many variants on these two games and many different and more complicated games as well, with more players and more rounds. They all show the same thing: people are not purely selfish individuals, rationally calculating how to maximize their benefits. They are also motivated by norms of cooperation, sharing and fairness.

Further undermining the theory that humans behave only in rational, self-serving ways are findings that show the very idea of "rational" decision making is flawed. Behavioral economics has found that when people consciously pursue their objectives, they don't understand probability, under- and over-estimate risk, are heavily influenced by how choices are framed and generally fail, in a wide variety of contexts, to "rationally" pursue their goals. These results were famously summarized by Richard Thaler and Cass Sunstein in their book *Nudge* and by Daniel Kahneman in his book *Thinking, Fast and Slow*.[23]

So we're not motivated purely by self-interest and we do a spotty job of pursuing that self-interest when we try. What does this say about standard models of the economy based on aggregating the assumed efficient, self-interested actions of millions and "proving" that everything works out for the best if those efficient, self-interested individuals are left alone? Nothing good.

And indeed nothing good has come out of applying that model, with varying degrees of intensity, for four decades. There has been no growth boom and no rapid rise in living standards. In fact, both overall economic growth and, especially, living standards growth have been relatively slow by historical standards, as noted in earlier chapters. And instead of unleashing a frenzy of creative solutions to long-standing economic problems, deregulated economies have just made most of them worse: more speculative bubbles, more risky investments, more inequality, more unemployment, more wage stagnation and so on. Finally, risky economic behavior, as we have seen, got completely out of control and the resulting financial meltdown sent the economy into the biggest nose-dive since the Great Depression.

It's fair to say the mainstream economic model now lies in ruins. Its core assumptions have been tested and found wanting.[24] Unleashing purely rational, purely self-interested individuals to do whatever they want has proved to be a recipe for stagnation at best and utter disaster at worst. And the reason is simple: these individuals don't exist and never will. Therefore, the market will never work as the current standard economic model says it should. Instead, an effective economics must accept the preferences and inclinations of actually existing people and reject the limits that imaginary perfect markets supposedly put on economic objectives.

That is what the opportunity state approach does. It builds on the aspects of human nature conservatives have ignored to achieve economic and social objectives the market alone cannot deliver. And in doing so, it reopens the question of the left's ultimate objective. Once, the goal of the left was essentially utopian—eliminating injustice and misery and creating a society where all people could flourish. Is that goal still possible?

REDISCOVERING UTOPIA

The twentieth century was a difficult century for the utopian vision. The Communist revolutions in Russia and China were supposed to usher in egalitarian utopias where all social needs were met by benevolent state planning. Instead, these Communist revolutions produced brutal authoritarian regimes in which privileged bureaucracies ruled over the masses and lagged far behind the advanced West in meeting social needs.

In the advanced West, social democrats pursued a gentler utopian ideal that envisioned an egalitarian society of abundance with social control of the economy and enhanced democracy in the workplace and throughout society. But the welfare state model ran into troubles starting in the 1970s as economic growth slowed and the inefficiencies of the system became ripe targets for conservative political forces. Support for the socialist ideal began to falter and the coup de grace was administered by the fall of the Soviet Union and the Eastern Europe states. Societies that had called themselves socialist turned their backs on the idea and embraced capitalism with gusto. Even Western European parties that still called themselves socialist abandoned any pretense that they were seeking to create an actual socialist society.

In America, there was also a utopian impulse, though it had its roots in more diffuse political traditions of liberalism and progressive reform. The idea here was that society could gradually perfect itself through a process of continuous reform that would weed out injustice and deliver prosperity for all. That idea came to a head with the Great Society of the 1960s but sputtered out soon thereafter, battered first by counter-cultural and political radicalism and then by a nascent conservatism fueled, as in Europe, by economic problems that exposed underlying governmental inefficiencies. Over time, the liberal movement backed far away from the Great Society and its expansive vision of social justice and became resolutely focused on maintaining American social programs or, at best, their modest expansion.

Counter-cultural and political radicalism had their own utopian impulses, of course. Visions of society ranging from participatory democracy (SDS) to communal bliss (hippies) to endless Marxist-Leninist revolution (Maoists) danced in the heads of young radicals in the 1960s. But such hubris did not survive the grimmer atmosphere of the 1970s, not to mention the pressures of the life cycle as these young radicals entered their thirties and forties.

As the left's utopian dreams faded, surging conservatives attacked vigorously. They argued that all of the left's failings—and especially their visions of a future society—were attributable to their fundamentally unrealistic beliefs about human nature. People were selfish and acquisitive, not cooperative and solidaristic as the left mistakenly believed. Therefore, the vision of society we should all strive for is a society without government and taxes in which self-ishness would be unleashed and individuals could shape their own destiny free of the oppressive hand of the state. This Ayn Rand–style libertarian utopia became an inspiration to legions of conservative activists.

There are still some true believers left in this utopia—some, indeed, hold elected office. But their dream of a perfectly unregulated capitalism has little mass appeal in our post–financial crisis world and will have less as the economy improves. The ideas underlying their vision of utopia have been tried and found wanting; their lease on utopia is up.

But the idea of utopia can and should live on. Utopia is fundamentally an expression of humanity's ability to dream of a better world. It provides—or should provide—inspiration to those seeking social change, highlighting a model for the society they seek to create. Without that inspiration, it is more difficult to sustain long-term commitment to substantial change, which inevitably saps energy from reform efforts. Reform, after all, is about taking steps to reach goals; a utopian vision helps you decide what those goals should be. Lacking robust goals, we have been experiencing a "sticky" status quo at the very time when large-scale change is necessary to deal with problems like climate change, slow growth, economic polarization and financial instability.

But things don't have to be this way. We are better situated than ever before to pursue a utopian dream that is reasonable and realistic and won't degenerate into authoritarianism or economic collapse.

So where is the new utopian vision to inspire today's left and its emerging postindustrial coalition? The first task will be to reawaken hope in the future by rejecting the limits and assumptions of the current debate.

The key limit is not that those on today's left still embrace a socialist or (in America) a "Great Society" utopia as a concrete goal. It is rather that they have given up on end goals altogether. It is as if those old utopias are the only ones the left could ever aspire to and, since those goals are no longer feasible or desirable, the left must do without. This leads to the uninspiring vision of a society that is, at best, a little bit better than the one we have today. Hardly the stuff of dreams and movements.

Moreover, the left finds itself drawn to an idealized past, since it now lacks a vision of a fundamentally better future. This generally takes the form of touting the Golden Age of the postwar welfare state, roughly the 1946–73 period, as some sort of model for society. It is true that wages and incomes rose much faster during that period than they have since, that there was far less economic inequality, that unions were much stronger and that basic institutions of the welfare state were not only safeguarded but expanded. But as utopia, that's pretty weak beer. And there is the inconvenient fact that this so-called Golden Age was not so golden for blacks, women, gays and other outsiders.

(Ironically, it is this aspect of the Golden Age—a stable, traditional social order—that is recalled with fondness by many on the right and held up on their side as a sort of model.)

Linked to this backward-looking viewpoint is a continued failure to grasp that the traditional working class—the bulwark of the postwar welfare state—is no longer the leading force for progress. Their place, as we have seen, has been taken by a diverse modernizing coalition that has quite a different sensibility than the traditional working class and is quite unmoved by appeals to an idealized past of happy workers with steadily rising living standards.

What would inspire them is quite different and it is here that the left will have to plough new ground. The left should embrace the new findings on human nature and economics, since they provide the basis for an expansive vision of humanity's future. And it should reject the pessimistic view of progress, so popular among today's left, that confuses current problems with long-term trends. It is true, as we have seen, that rising inequality in the United States and other countries has limited the benefits of economic growth, as well as slowed that growth. It is also true that globalization has produced its share of losers in the United States and that globally many nations are still mired in poverty. And it is certainly true that world economic progress has brought with it serious climate problems. But economic growth and globalization as long-term trends are still far more beneficial than harmful, a fact that resonates with this emerging coalition, even if the traditional working class no longer believes it.

A NEW UTOPIAN VISION FOR THE LEFT

A new utopian vision for the left's emerging coalition will take some time to consolidate but it will surely be very different from left utopias of the past. It is likely to include the following features. First, there will be a commitment to abundance.

This means the left will discard its flirtation with anti-growth ideologies and fully embrace the idea that material abundance is a very good thing and should be extended to all. It is only those that already have it that are inclined to downplay its importance. In this century, it will be within our capabilities for virtually everyone to not only live longer, healthier lives, with their basic needs met, but also have considerable additional resources for consumption of the good things in life, including travel, recreation and, yes, the various "gadgets" that make life more interesting and entertaining. The left should therefore aspire to a society where that is a reality. The rapidly growing upper middle class has such a life—the left's vision should see that standard of living diffusing throughout society and the world.

Closely linked to this aspect of the left's utopian vision will be a re-embrace of technology. Technological advance is the key to generalized abundance, so a vision of a bright technological future and limitless progress is essential. It is not necessary to envision a future exactly like *The Jetsons*— flying cars, while a nice thought, can be dispensed with— but it *is* necessary to rediscover the optimistic attitude toward future scientific progress that was characteristic of that era. Tremendous progress is indeed possible and will produce lives for the overwhelming majority that are richer, easier and more interesting and exciting than those today. The exact wonders that will become part of people's everyday lives are, of course, very difficult to predict. But there will be wonders.

Technological progress will also have a central role in another aspect of the left's vision—a green world where the environment is safeguarded and global warming is held in check. A sustainable world underpinned by advanced technology that provides cheap, clean energy, mitigates greenhouse gas damage and solves resource-depletion problems is eminently possible. And we won't achieve that sustainable world without those advances, contrary to those eco-pessimists who advocate stopping or even reversing economic growth and see science as an enemy. A left vision of a better world is both green and rooted in advanced science and technology.

A left vision of a better world is also a global, interconnected world. Globalization produces some problems, many of which have been poorly managed in advanced countries, but it is neither possible nor desirable to stop it. It is ultimately a powerful force for a richer, more equal world where more and more people lead fulfilling lives, free from immiserating material constraints, and where global exchange of knowledge and culture uplifts everyone. The left has a history of rhetorically embracing global values ("the workers have no country," "all men are brothers") but a left vision for the twenty-first century will go beyond mere rhetoric to embrace the reality of a globalized world, where all can and should rise together.

This means explicitly rejecting the idea that there is an intrinsically disadvantageous tradeoff between the welfare of the West and the welfare of the rest of the world. Instead, "the rise of the rest," as Charles Kenny puts it, is a tremendous opportunity for the West to connect to the markets and talents of a rising global middle class and set humanity on a path to universal enrichment.[25] The "good society" of the future will be a global society, rather than a country-by-country affair.

Closely related to this, the left will aim for a world where racial and gender equality are worldwide realities, where sexual orientation is a non-prejudicial, individual affair and where tolerance of others from different cultural, religious or national backgrounds is the rule. The level of progress in these areas in the last 50 years should make us very optimistic that such a world is possible. Of course, we are very aware of the many instances in which the world currently falls short of these ideals, but that in and of itself is a sign of progress. These ideals are very widely held and more so with every passing year, so these shortcomings increasingly attract public attention and disapproval, making them more likely to be remedied.

Universal and deepened democracy will be another aspect of the left's vision for the twenty-first century. Universal suffrage, with freedoms of the press, association, speech, etc., should be and can be the core governmental form in every country. In addition, the advance of information technology should be leveraged to provide citizens with far greater access to the workings of government and ease the costs of political participation across the world.

Key to these advances will be the left's vision of an educated world. High levels of education facilitate democracy, progressive social values, global openness, green preferences and technological achievement. Great progress has already been made but it is now appropriate to aspire to not just universal literacy but universal tertiary (college) education. That does not mean that everyone will necessarily have a four-year college degree, in the American sense. It means rather that all will attain a secondary education and then go as far in the tertiary realm as their interests and talents can take them. The elimination of barriers to this level of achievement will be central to the left's vision of the good society.

Note this vision does not include an embrace of "socialism"—much less a planned economy—and implicitly assumes that capitalism will continue in some form with a large role for the market. The key question is not "whether capitalism?" but rather "what form of capitalism?" That form will be the advanced opportunity state that comes as close as possible to the ideal of equal opportunity for all. This will be achieved via a robust role for government in promoting high educational attainment, maintaining full employment, making necessary public investments, providing social insurance and generally driving strong, well-distributed economic growth.

Of course, such a society will not be perfect. But perfection is not the point. The goal is to make society as close as it reasonably can be to the left's new utopian vision, while making no heroic assumptions about the infinite malleability of humanity or the functionality of an economy that ignores market signals. The left's watchword should be feasibility, not ideological consistency. Call it *pragmatic utopianism*.

Part of this approach is recognizing that you will never entirely get to your ultimate goals. Indeed, this type of utopianism is a continuous process, a never-ending quest to improve society and bring it closer to these goals. It is the signature of the optimistic leftist and of a twenty-first century that will be far, far better than you think. We live in extraordinary times; the left can and will make them extraordinarily good for humanity.

ACKNOWLEDGMENTS

This book is the product of many years of thinking, reading and discussion. Along the way, I have benefitted from the insights of many people, not least my colleagues at the Center for American Progress, particularly Rob Griffin, John Halpin and David Madland.

In addition, I have benefitted from personal conversations and exchanges with Jared Bernstein, William Frey, Benjamin Friedman, John Judis, Lane Kenworthy and Stephen Rose, all of whose writings have influenced me greatly. Other key intellectual influences on this book include Mark Blyth, Samuel Bowles, Ronald Brownstein, John Cassidy, Jonathan Chait, Angus Deaton, Brad DeLong, E.J. Dionne, Stanley Greenberg, Michael Grunwald, Herbert

Gintis, Jacob Hacker, Charles Kenny, Paul Krugman, Michael Levi, Angus Maddison, Mariana Mazzucato, Branko Milanovic, Joel Mokyr, Ramez Naam, Paul Pierson, Steven Pinker, Thomas Piketty, Noam Scheiber, Robert Skidelsky, Noah Smith, Joseph Stiglitz, Lawrence Summers, David Sloan Wilson, Edward O. Wilson and Simon Wren-Lewis. I could not have written this book without the tremendous work of these scholars.

Indeed, to the extent this work offers useful insights into our collective future, they deserve a great deal of the credit. Conversely, to the extent the book seems the unhinged ravings of a lunatic, that's all on me.

Finally, a big shout out to my editor at St. Martin's, Elisabeth Dyssegaard, who believed in this book and hounded me until I wrote it. And to the greatest reasons in my life for optimism: my wife, Robin Allen, and my children, Lauren and Ian Teixeira, who were unflaggingly supportive and listened tolerantly as I test-drove many of these arguments at the dinner table.

NOTES

CHAPTER ONE

1. Author's analysis of Maddison Project historical GDP data series, http://www.ggdc.net/maddison/maddison-project/home.htm. Cited hereafter as author's analysis of Maddison Project data.
2. Benjamin M. Friedman, *The Moral Consequences of Economic Growth* (New York: Vintage, 2006), 115. The historical approach in this chapter and my general perspective on economic growth and the left owe a great deal to Friedman's magisterial work.
3. Author's analysis of Maddison Project data.
4. Peter H. Lindert and Jeffrey G. Williamson, *Unequal Gains: American Growth and Inequality Since 1700* (Princeton, NJ: Princeton University Press, 2016), 120, 166–173. Note, however, that outside of a sharp rise in the incomes of the very wealthy, there was not a generalized increase in income inequality within the rest of the population, as happened in America before 1860 and after 1970.

5. Friedman, *The Moral Consequences of Economic Growth*, 116.
6. For a good political account of this era, see James Sundquist, *Dynamics of the Party System: Alignment and Realignment of Political Parties in the United States* (Washington, DC: Brookings Institution Press, 1983).
7. Ibid., 163.
8. Author's analysis of Maddison Project data.
9. These are Bureau of Labor Statistics economist Stanley Lebergott's historical estimates, found in "Annual Estimates of Unemployment in the United States, 1900–1954," in National Bureau of Economic Research, *The Measurement and Behavior of Unemployment* (NBER, 1957), http://www.nber.org/chapters/c2644 .pdf. Different figures were offered in Christina Romer, "Spurious Volatility in Historical Unemployment Statistics," *Journal of Political Economy* 94, no. 1 (1986), 1–37, which show less volatility than Lebergott's but tell basically the same story. See also these posts in the blog Social Democracy for the 21st Century for good summaries of the descriptive data in these and other historical unemployment series: http://socialdemocracy21stcentury.blog spot.com/search?q=unemployment.
10. Friedman, *The Moral Consequences of Economic Growth*, 132.
11. James Chace, *1912: Wilson, Roosevelt, Taft and Debs—The Election That Changed the Country* (New York: Simon and Schuster, 2004), 167.
12. Author's analysis of Maddison Project data.
13. Thomas Piketty, *Capital in the Twenty-First Century* (Cambridge, MA: Harvard University Press, 2014), 24; and Lindert and Williamson, *Unequal Gains*, 197–198.
14. Sundquist, *Dynamics of the Party System*, 189–190.
15. Author's analysis of Maddison Project data.
16. Author's analysis of Office of Management and Budget (OMB), Historical Tables, Budget of the U.S. Government, Fiscal Year 2011 (Executive Office of the President, 2010). Public investment is defined as nonmilitary expenditures on infrastructure, research and development, and education and training. Cited hereafter as author's analysis of OMB data.
17. Robert Pollin and Dean Baker, "Public Investment, Industrial

Policy and U.S. Economic Renewal," Political Economy Research Institute and Center for Economic and Policy Research, Amherst, MA, and Washington, DC, 2009, http://www.peri.umass.edu/fileadmin/pdf/working_papers/working_papers_201-250/WP211.pdf.

18. Author's analysis of Maddison Project data.

19. Robert Skidelsky, *Keynes: The Return of the Master* (New York: Public Affairs, 2010), 118.

20. Author's analysis of Current Population Survey (CPS) historical family income data, http://www.census.gov/data/tables/time-series/demo/income-poverty/historical-income-families.html. Cited hereafter as author's analysis of CPS historical family income data.

21. Lawrence Mishel, John Bivens, Elise Gould and Heidi Shierholz, *The State of Working America, 12th Edition* (Ithaca, NY: Cornell University Press, 2012), 67.

22. This gain may be somewhat understated. Analysis by the Congressional Budget Office that takes into account changes in household size, taxes and benefits suggests greater, though still comparatively modest, gains over this time period. See the discussion in chapter 4.

23. Author's analysis of CPS historical family income data.

24. Chad Stone, Danilo Trisi, Arloc Sherman and Brandon DeBot, "A Guide to Statistics on Historical Trends in Income Inequality," Center for Budget and Policy Priorities, October 26, 2015, http://www.cbpp.org/sites/default/files/atoms/files/11-28-11pov_0.pdf.

25. Pre-1973 results from author's analysis of Maddison Project data; post-1973 results from author's analysis of Measuring-Worth, historical GDP data, https://www.measuringworth.com/growth/.

26. Skidelsky, *Keynes: The Return of the Master*, 117–118. Note that Skidelsky's data actually leave out the relatively high unemployment 1973–79 transition period as well as the high unemployment Great Recession years.

27. Author's analysis of OMB data.

28. Polling and Baker, "Public Investment, Industrial Policy and U.S. Economic Renewal."

29. American Society of Civil Engineers, *2013 Report Card for America's Infrastructure Needs,* http://www.infrastructurereportcard .org/a/#p/grade-sheet/americas-infrastructure-investment-needs. Reston, VA, 2013.
30. Kevin Phillips, *The Emerging Republican Majority* (New York: Arlington House, 1969).
31. Ruy Teixeira and Joel Rogers, *America's Forgotten Majority: Why the White Working Class Still Matters* (New York: Basic, 2000), 6.
32. Ibid., 32.
33. Ibid.
34. See Friedman, *The Moral Consequences of Economic Growth,* chapters 9–11, for detailed case studies of Britain, France and Germany and various ways they fit this pattern.

CHAPTER TWO

1. Bernhard Wessels, Jan Engels and Gero Maass, "Demographic Change and Progressive Political Strategy in Germany," Center for American Progress: Global Progress, April, 2011, https:// cdn.americanprogress.org/wp-content/uploads/issues/2011 /04/pdf/germany_report.pdf.
2. Odd Guteland, "Demographic Change and Progressive Political Strategy in Sweden," Center for American Progress: Global Progress, April, 2011, https://cdn.americanprogress.org/wp-content /uploads/issues/2011/04/pdf/sweden_report_draft.pdf.
3. Wessels, et al., "Demographic Change and Progressive Political Strategy in Germany."
4. Angus Maddison, *Contours of the World Economy, 1–2030 AD: Essays in Macroeconomic History* (Oxford: Oxford University Press, 2007), Table 2.5.
5. Author's analysis of Bureau of Labor Statistics (BLS) occupation and industry data, industry employment and output projections to 2024, December, 2015. Available at: http://www.bls .gov/emp/ep_table_201.htm. Cited hereafter as author's analysis of BLS.

6. Maddison, *Contours of the World Economy, 1–2030 AD.*
7. Bureau of Labor Statistics, "Union Members—2015," January 28, 2016, http://www.bls.gov/news.release/pdf/union2.pdf.
8. Lane Kenworthy, *Progress for the Poor* (Oxford: Oxford University Press, 2011), https://lanekenworthy.net/books/.
9. Author's analysis of data in Gerassimos Maschonas, "Lower Classes or Middle Classes?: Socialism and Its Changing Constituencies in Great Britain, Sweden and Denmark," presentation to Council for European Studies, March 5, 2008; and Anthony Painter, "The New Pluralist Imperative in Britain: Demographic Change and Progressive Political Strategy in the United Kingdom," Center for American Progress: Global Progress, April, 2011, https://cdn.americanprogress.org/wp-content/uploads/issues/2011/04/pdf/uk_report.pdf.
10. Ron Lesthaeghe, "The Unfolding Story of the Second Demographic Transition," Population Studies Center, University of Michigan, January 2010. Available at: http://www.psc.isr.umich.edu/pubs/pdf/rr10-696.pdf.
11. Wessels, et al., "Demographic Change and Progressive Political Strategy in Germany."
12. Author's analysis of BLS data.
13. Anthony P. Carnevale and Stephen J. Rose, *The Economy Goes to College: The Hidden Promise of Higher Education in the Post-Industrial Service Economy*, report for the Center on Education and the Workforce, Georgetown University, 2015, https://cew.georgetown.edu/cew-reports/the-economy-goes-to-college/.
14. Hans Anker, René Cuperus and Pim Paulusma, "A Systemic Meltdown?: Demographic Change and Progressive Political Strategy in the Netherlands," Center for American Progress: Global Progress, April, 2011, https://cdn.americanprogress.org/wp-content/uploads/issues/2011/04/pdf/netherlands_report.pdf.
15. Alain Richard, Olivier Ferrand, Bruno Jeanbart, Alain Bergounioux, Gérard Le Gall, Romain Prudent and Etienne Schweisguth, "Demographic Change and Progressive Political Strategy in France: Defining a Coalition for 2012?" Center for

American Progress: Global Progress, April 2011, https://cdn
.americanprogress.org/wp-content/uploads/issues/2011/04
/pdf/france_report.pdf.

16. Data in this paragraph from author's analysis of 1940–2000
Census data and 2014 Current Population Survey Annual Social and Economic Supplement education data, http://www
.census.gov/hhes/socdemo/education/data/cps/2014/tables
.html.

17. Author's analysis of post-2000 national exit poll data. National Election Pool Surveys, conducted by Edison Media
Research.

18. Data in this paragraph based on author's analysis of University of Michigan American National Election Studies data, available at http://www.electionstudies.org/studypages/download
/datacenter_all_NoData.php. Data on occupational breakdown of the vote not available for 2008 due to confidentiality
restrictions. A reasonable estimate based on historical patterns would be around 68 percent support among professionals for Obama in 2008. For more discussion of professionals'
political evolution, see John B. Judis and Ruy Teixeira, *The
Emerging Democratic Majority* (New York: Scribner, 2002),
chapter 2.

19. The 2008 election was no exception to this pattern. Using those
with a postgraduate education as a proxy for this group (the
exit polls have no occupation question), Obama received
58 percent to 40 percent support, which is up from 55 percent
to 44 percent for Kerry in 2004 and 52 percent to 44 percent for
Gore in 2000. In 2012, Obama received 55-42 support over
Romney and in 2016 Clinton carried these voters over Trump
by 58–37.

20. Author's analysis of BLS data.

21. Pablo Beramendi, Silja Häusermann, Herbert Kitschelt and
Hanspeter Kriesi, "Introduction: The Politics of Advanced
Capitalism" in Pablo Beramendi, Silja Häusermann, Herbert
Kitschelt and Hanspeter Kriesi, eds., *The Politics of Advanced
Capitalism* (New York: Cambridge University Press, 2015).

22. Author's analysis of European Social Survey (ESS) data, round 7, 2014, http://www.europeansocialsurvey.org/data/download .html?r=7. Cited hereafter as author's analysis of 2014 ESS data.
23. Other examples: In the 2011 Finnish election, the figures were 12 and 14 points; and in the 2014 Swedish election, the support advantage for the greens and left socialists was 10 points among both college-educated and professional voters. All figures from author's analysis of 2014 ESS data.
24. Out of 11 countries examined from the 2014 ESS. The other four are Denmark, France, Norway and Great Britain.
25. Centrist parties politically position themselves between left and conservative parties. Many though not all of these centrist parties affiliate with the European parliamentary group Alliance of Liberals and Democrats for Europe (ALDE). Conversely, some of the ALDE parties (e.g., the Netherlands VVD) are really positioned as conservative parties and are classified as such.
26. Author's analysis of 2014 ESS data.
27. Ruy Teixeira, William H. Frey and Robert Griffin, "States of Change: The Demographic Evolution of the American Electorate, 1974–2060," Center for American Progress and American Enterprise Institute, February, 2015, https://cdn.americanprogress .org/wp-content/uploads/2015/02/SOC-report1.pdf.
28. Using the Census definition: minorities are those that select one race and for whom that one race is not white *or* who are multiracial *or* who are Hispanic.
29. Data in this paragraph from Anthony Painter, "The New Pluralist Imperative in Britain"; Anker, et al., "A Systemic Meltdown?"; Ferran Martínez i Coma, "Demographic Change and Progressive Political Strategy in Spain," Center for American Progress: Global Progress, April 2011, https://cdn.americanprogress.org /wp-content/uploads/issues/2011/04/pdf/spain_report.pdf; and Richard, et al., "Demographic Change and Progressive Political Strategy in France: Defining a Coalition for 2012?"
30. See Wessels, et al., "Demographic Change and Progressive Political Strategy in Germany"; Richard, et al., "Demographic

Change and Progressive Political Strategy in France: Defining a Coalition for 2012?"; and Painter, "The New Progressive Imperative in Britain."

31. Author's analysis of 2014 ESS data.
32. Author's analysis of national exit polls, 2008 and 2012.
33. Teixeira, et al., "States of Change: The Demographic Evolution of the American Electorate, 1974–2060"; and Robert Griffin, William H. Frey and Ruy Teixeira, "The Demographic Evolution of the American Electorate, 1980–2060 Interactive," https://www.americanprogress.org/issues/progressive-movement/news/2015/02/24/107166/interactive-the-demographic-evolution-of-the-american-electorate-1980-2060/.
34. See the various survey reports from Women's Voices Women Vote Action Fund, http://www.wvwvaf.org/research/.
35. Teixeira, et al., "States of Change: The Demographic Evolution of the American Electorate, 1974–2060."
36. Painter, "The New Progressive Imperative in Britain"; and Anker, et al., "A Systemic Meltdown?"
37. Author's analysis of 2012 national exit poll.
38. Anker, et al., "A Systemic Meltdown?"; and Richard, et al., "Demographic Change and Progressive Political Strategy in France: Defining a Coalition for 2012?"
39. Pew Research Center, *America's Changing Religious Landscape,* Pew Research Center, May 12, 2015.
40. Author's analysis of 2012 National Election Pool national exit poll, conducted by Edison Media Research.
41. Author's analysis of 2014 ESS data.
42. Author's analysis of 2014 ESS data.
43. Teixeira, et al., "States of Change: The Demographic Evolution of the American Electorate, 1974–2060."
44. See Pew Research Center, *The Whys and Hows of Generation Research,* Pew Research Center, September 3, 2015.
45. Author's analysis of 2008 and 2012 national exit polls.
46. Data in this paragraph from author's analysis of 2014 ESS data.

47. See Benjamin I. Page and Lawrence R. Jacobs, *Class War?: What Americans Really Think about Economic Inequality* (Chicago: University of Chicago Press, 2009); Leslie McCall, *The Undeserving Rich: American Beliefs about Inequality, Opportunity and Redistribution* (New York: Cambridge University Press, 2013); and Ron Haskins and Isabel V. Sawhill, *Creating an Opportunity Society* (Washington, DC: Brookings University Press, 2009).

48. See Anthony Giddens, *The Third Way: The Renewal of Social Democracy* (Cambridge, UK: Polity Press, 1998).

CHAPTER THREE

1. Branko Milanovic, *The Haves and Have-Nots: a Brief and Idiosyncratic History of Global Inequality* (New York: Basic, 2011), 109–114; Jonathan Sperber, *Karl Marx: A Nineteenth Century Life* (New York: Norton, 2013), 419–463; Thomas Piketty, *Capital in the Twenty-First Century* (Cambridge, MA: Harvard University Press, 2014), 7–11.

2. Piketty, *Capital in the Twenty-First Century*, 13–15.

3. Anthony Giddens, *The Third Way: The Renewal of Social Democracy* (Malden, MA: Blackwell, 1998).

4. Paul Krugman, *End This Depression Now!* (New York: Norton, 2012).

5. Carmen DeNavas-Walt and Bernadette D. Proctor, *Income and Poverty in the United States: 2014* (Washington, DC: US Census Bureau, September 2015), 23, http://www.census.gov /content/dam/Census/library/publications/2015/demo/p60 -252.pdf.

6. Piketty, *Capital in the Twenty-First Century*.

7. Ibid., 304–335.

8. Ibid., 23.

9. See Jonathan D. Ostry, Andrew Berg and Charalambos G. Tsangarides, "Redistribution, Inequality and Growth," IMF Staff Discussion Note, April, 2014, https://www.imf.org/external

/pubs/ft/sdn/2014/sdn1402.pdf; Andrew G. Berg and Jonathan D. Ostry, "Inequality and Unsustainable Growth: Two Sides of the Same Coin?" IMF Staff Discussion Note, April 8, 2011, https://www.imf.org/external/pubs/cat/longres.aspx?sk =24686.0; Era Dabla-Norris, Kalpana Kochhar, Nujin Suphaphi- phat, Frantisek Ricka, and Evridiki Tsounta, "Causes and Con- sequences of Income Inequality: A Global Perspective," IMF Staff Discussion Note, June 2015, http://www.imf.org/external /pubs/ft/sdn/2015/sdn1513.pdf; OECD, "Focus on Inequality and Growth," OECD Directorate for Employment, Labour and Social Affairs, December 2014, https://www.oecd.org/social /Focus-Inequality-and-Growth-2014.pdf; Jared Bernstein, "The Impact of Inequality on Growth," Center for American Pro- gress, December, 2013, https://www.americanprogress.org /wp-content/uploads/2013/12/BernsteinInequality.pdf; Heather Boushey and Carter C. Price, "How Are Economic Inequality and Growth Connected?: A Review of Recent Re- search" Washington Center on Equitable Growth, October, 2014, http://equitablegrowth.org/wp-content/uploads/2014 /10/100914-ineq-growth.pdf.

10. Claudia Goldin and Lawrence F. Katz, *The Race between Educa- tion and Technology* (Cambridge, MA: Harvard University Press, 2008).

11. For a crisp presentation of the case for full employment, see Jared Bernstein, *The Reconnection Agenda: Reuniting Growth and Prosperity* (Amazon Digital Services, 2015), 44–64.

12. For extensive discussion of this point, see Lane Kenworthy, *So- cial Democratic America* (New York: Oxford University Press, 2014), 49–72.

13. Piketty, *Capital in the Twenty-First Century*, 493–514; Peter Diamond and Emmanuel Saez, "The Case for a Progressive Tax: From Basic Research to Policy Recommendations," Berkeley, CA, CESifo Working Paper 3548, August, 2011, http://eml.berkeley.edu//~saez/diamond-saezJEP11opttax .pdf.

14. Mariana Mazzucato, *The Entrepreneurial State: Debunking*

Public Vs. Private Sector Myths (New York: Anthem Press, 2014), 57–71.

15. Ibid., 87–112.

16. Jacob S. Hacker and Paul Pierson, "Why Technological Innovation Relies on Government Support," *The Atlantic* (March 28, 2016), http://www.theatlantic.com/politics/archive/2016/03/andy-grove-government-technology/475626/; Hacker and Pierson, *American Amnesia: How the War on Government Led Us to Forget What Made America Prosper* (New York: Simon & Schuster, 2016), 45–69.

17. Mazzucato, *The Entrepreneurial State*, 63.

18. Kenworthy, *Social Democratic America*, 10–11.

19. Christopher Ellis and James A. Stimson, *Ideology in America* (New York: Cambridge University Press, 2012), xiv.

20. For much more on this and other objections to the feasibility of expanded government, see Kenworthy, *Social Democratic America*, 149–176.

21. Pre-1973 results from author's analysis of Maddison Project historical GDP data series, http://www.ggdc.net/maddison/maddison-project/home.htm; post-1973 results from author's analysis of MeasuringWorth historical GDP data, https://www.measuringworth.com/growth/.

22. J. Bradford DeLong, "Inequality, Prosperity, Growth, and Well-Being in America," Washington Center for Equitable Growth: Equitablog, October 21, 2015, http://equitablegrowth.org/equitablog/inequality-prosperity-growth-and-well-being-in-america/.

23. I am indebted in this discussion to Mark Blyth, *Austerity: The History of a Dangerous Idea* (New York: Oxford University Press, 2013).

24. See Henry Farrell and John Quiggin, "Consensus, Dissensus and Economic Ideas: The Rise and Fall of Keynesianism During the Economic Crisis," March 9, 2012, http://www.henryfarrell.net/Keynes.pdf for a blow-by-blow description of how this happened.

25. Blyth, *Austerity*, 178–226.

26. Paul Krugman, "The Austerity Delusion," *The Guardian*, April 29, 2015, http://www.theguardian.com/business/ng-interactive /2015/apr/29/the-austerity-delusion; Krugman, "Austerity's Grim Legacy," *New York Times*, November 6, 2015, http://www .nytimes.com/2015/11/06/opinion/austeritys-grim-legacy.html? _r=0.

27. Eurostat, "Real GDP Growth Rate," http://ec.europa.eu/eurostat /tgm /table .do?tab=table &init=1 &language=en &pcode =tec00115&plugin=1, accessed July 30, 2016.

28. Thomas Cooley, Ben Griffy and Peter Rupert, "Unequal Growth But Evidence of Improvement in Europe," *European Economic Snapshot*, May 9, 2016, https://europeansnapshot.com /2016/05/09/unequal-growth-but-evidence-of-improvement -in-europe/.

29. Antonio Fatas and Lawrence H. Summers, "The Permanent Effects of Fiscal Consolidation," National Bureau of Economic Research: NBER Working Paper No. 22374, June 2016, http:// www.nber.org/papers/w22374.

30. Lawrence Summers, "Global Economy: The Case for Expansion," *Financial Times*, October 7, 2015, http://www.ft.com/cms /s/0/1e912316-6b88-11e5-8171-ba1968cf791a.html#axzz4Fvt ECmCy.

31. Brad DeLong, "A Reader's Guide to the Secular Stagnation Debate," Washington Center for Equitable Growth: Equitablog, October 17, 2015, http://equitablegrowth.org/equitablog/a -readers-guide-to-the-secular-stagnation-debate-the-honest -broker-for-the-week-of-october-12-2015/; Brad DeLong, "The Scary Debate Over Secular Stagnation," *The Milken Institute Review*, Fourth Quarter, 2015, http://delong.typepad.com/milken -review-secular-stagnation-34-51-mr68.pdf.

32. International Monetary Fund, "World Economic Outlook: Legacies, Clouds, Uncertainties," October 2014, 75–114, http://www .imf.org/external/pubs/ft/weo/2014/02/pdf/text.pdf.

33. Bernstein, *The Reconnection Agenda*, 47.

34. Jared Bernstein, "The Full Employment Productivity Multiplier," *The Washington Post*, February 4, 2016, https://www

.washingtonpost.com/posteverything/wp/2016/02/04/the
-full-employment-productivity-multiplier/.

35. DeLong, "The Scary Debate about Secular Stagnation."

36. Robert Pollin, Heidi Garrett-Peltier, James Heintz, and Bracken Hendricks, "Green Growth: A U.S. Program for Controlling Climate Change and Expanding Job Opportunities," Washington, DC: Center for American Progress, September 2014, 198–235.

37. Ramez Naam, "The Limits of the Earth, Part 1: Problems," *Scientific American*, April 17, 2013, http://blogs.scientificamerican.com/guest-blog/the-limits-of-the-earth-part-1-problems/.

38. Ramez Naam, *The Infinite Resource: The Power of Ideas on a Finite Planet* (Lebanon, NH: University Press of New England, 2013).

39. Naam, "The Limits of the Earth, Part 1."

40. Ramez Naam, "The Limits of the Earth, Part 2: Expanding the Limits," *Scientific American*, April 18, 2013, http://blogs.scientificamerican.com/guest-blog/the-limits-of-the-earth-part-2-expanding-the-limits/.

41. Ralf Fücks, *Green Growth, Smart Growth: A New Approach to Economics, Innovation and the Environment* (New York: Anthem Press, 2015).

42. Joel Mokyr, "Interview with Joel Mokyr," Goldman Sachs: Top of Mind, October 5, 2015, http://www.goldmansachs.com/our-thinking/pages/macroeconomic-insights-folder/the-productivity-paradox/report.pdf.

43. See, for example, Peter H. Diamandis and Steven Kotler, *Abundance: The Future Is Better Than You Think* (New York: Free Press, 2012); and Ray Kurzweil, *The Singularity Is Near: When Humans Transcend Biology* (New York: Penguin, 2005).

44. Leigh Phillips, *Austerity Ecology & the Collapse-Porn Addicts: A Defence of Growth, Progress, Industry and Stuff* (Washington, DC: Zero Books, 2014), 144.

45. Robert Gordon, "Is U.S. Economic Growth Over? Faltering Innovation Confronts the Six Headwinds," NBER Working Paper No. 18315, 2012; and Robert J. Gordon, *The Rise and Fall*

of American Growth: The U.S. Standard of Living since the Civil War (Princeton, NJ: Princeton University Press, 2016).

46. Mokyr, "Interview with Joel Mokyr."

47. Ramez Naam, "How Cheap Can Solar Get: Very Cheap Indeed," rameznaam.com, August 10, 2015, http://rameznaam.com/2015 /08/10/how-cheap-can-solar-get-very-cheap-indeed/.

48. Michio Kaku, *Visions: How Science Will Revolutionize the 21st Century* (New York: Anchor Books, 1997).

49. Joel Mokyr, Chris Vickers, and Nicolas L. Ziebarth, "The History of Technological Anxiety and the Future of Economic Growth: Is This Time Different?" *Journal of Economic Perspectives*, 29, no. 3 (Summer 2015), 31–50, http://pubs.aeaweb.org /doi/pdfplus/10.1257/jep.29.3.31.

50. Kevin Drum, "Robots Aren't Here Yet, But That Doesn't Mean They Never Will Be," *Mother Jones*, February 18, 2014, http:// www.motherjones.com/kevin-drum/2014/02/robots-arent -here-yet-doesnt-mean-they-never-will-be.

51. Kevin Drum, "Welcome Robot Overlords. Please Don't Fire Us?" *Mother Jones*, May/June, 2013, http://www.motherjones .com/media/2013/05/robots-artificial-intelligence-jobs -automation.

52. Anthony P. Carnevale and Stephen J. Rose, *The Economy Goes to College: The Hidden Promise of Higher Education in the Post-Industrial Service Economy*, Center on Education and the Workforce, Georgetown University, 2015, 87.

53. Drum, "Welcome Robot Overlords. Please Don't Fire Us?"

54. Martin Ford, *Rise of the Robots: Technology and the Threat of a Jobless Future* (New York: Basic, 2015).

55. Stephen Rose, "Don't Fear the Robots," *Washington Monthly*, September 29, 2015, http://washingtonmonthly.com/2015/09 /29/dont-fear-the-robots/.

56. Max Roser, "World Poverty," *Our World in Data*, https:// ourworldindata.org/world-poverty/, accessed July 31, 2016; Marcio Cruz, James Foster, Bryce Quillin and Philip Schellekens, "Ending Extreme Poverty and Sharing Prosperity: Progress and Policies," World Bank Policy Research Note, October, 2015.

57. Branko Milanovic, "Global Income Inequality in Numbers: in History and Now," *Global Policy* 4, no. 2 (May 2013), 202.

58. World Health Organization, *World health statistics 2013,* World Health Organization, 2013, http://www.who.int/gho/publications /world_health_statistics/EN_WHS2013_Full.pdf.

59. Matt Ridley, *The Rational Optimist: How Prosperity Evolves* (New York: HarperCollins, 2010), 15.

60. Charles Kenny, *The Upside of Down: Why the Rise of the Rest Is Good for the West* (New York: Basic, 2013), 25.

61. For a thorough explication of Marx's views in this area, see Bill Warren, *Imperialism: Pioneer of Capitalism* (London: Verso, 1980).

62. Stephen Rose, "The Truth about Trade and Job Losses," *Washington Monthly,* March 18, 2016, http://washingtonmonthly.com /2016/03/18/the-truth-about-trade-and-job-losses/.

63. Robert Rowthorn and Ramana Ramaswamy, "Deindustrialization—Its Causes and Implications," Washington, DC: International Monetary Fund, September 1997, https://www.imf .org/EXTERNAL/PUBS/FT/ISSUES10/issue10.pdf; Christopher Kollmeyer, "Explaining Deindustrialization: How Affluence, Productivity Growth, and Globalization Diminish Manufacturing Employment," *American Journal of Sociology* 114, no. 6 (May 2009): 1644–74, https://instruct.uwo.ca/geog/9322 /Kollmeyer.pdf.

64. David H. Autor, David Dorn and Gordon H. Hanson, "The China Shock: Learning from Labor Market Adjustment to Large Changes in Trade," National Bureau of Economic Research, NBER Working Paper No. 21906, January 2016, http://www .nber.org/papers/w21906.

65. Kenny, *The Upside of Down,* 58, 154.

CHAPTER FOUR

1. Max Roser, "World Poverty," *Our World in Data,* https://our worldindata.org/world-poverty/, accessed July 31, 2016.

2. Brad DeLong, "Estimating World GDP, One Million B.C.— Present," j-bradford-delong.net, May 24, 1998, http://www.j

-bradford-delong.net/TCEH/1998_Draft/World_GDP /Estimating_World_GDP.html.

3. Working Party on Climate, Investment and Development, "Long-Term Economic Growth And Environmental Pressure: Reference Scenarios For Future Global Projections," Environment Directorate, Organisation for Economic Co-operation and Development, September 26, 2012, http://www.oecd.org /officialdocuments/publicdisplaydocumentpdf/?cote=ENV /EPOC/WPCID(2012)6&docLanguage=En.

4. Max Roser, "Life Expectancy," *Our World in Data*, https:// ourworldindata.org/life-expectancy/, accessed July 31, 2016.

5. Matt Ridley, *The Rational Optimist: How Prosperity Evolves* (New York: HarperCollins, 2010), 14.

6. See Robert J. Gordon, *The Rise and Fall of American Growth: The U.S. Standard of Living since the Civil War* (Princeton, NJ: Princeton University Press, 2016), for copious detail.

7. Ridley, *The Rational Optimist*, 16–17.

8. The definitive treatment of the decline in violence is Steven Pinker, *The Better Angels of Our Nature: Why Violence Has Declined* (New York: Viking, 2011).

9. Steven Pinker, "A History of Violence; We're Getting Nicer Every Day," *New Republic*, March 19, 2007, https://newrepublic .com/article/64340/history-violence-were-getting-nicer-every -day.

10. Bas van Leeuwen and Jieli van Leeuwen-Li, "Education Since 1820," in Jan Luiten van Zanden, Joerg Baten, Marco Mira d'Ercole, Auke Rijpma, Conal Smith and Marcel Timmer, eds., *How Was Life? Global Well-being since 1820* (OECD Publishing, 2014), 87–100, http://adapt.it/englishbulletin/wp/wp-content /uploads/2014/10/oecd_2_10_2014.pdf; Angus Maddison, "Causal Influences on Productivity Performance 1820–1992: A Global Perspective," *Journal of Productivity Analysis* (November 1997): 325–360.

11. Max Roser, "Literacy," *Our World in Data*, https://ourworld-indata.org/literacy/, accessed July 31, 2016.

12. World Bank, "Gross enrollment ratio, tertiary, both sexes,"

http://data.worldbank.org/indicator/SE.TER.ENRR, accessed August 1, 2016.

13. Joel Mokyr, "Interview with Joel Mokyr," Goldman Sachs: Top of Mind, October 5, 2015, http://www.goldmansachs.com /our-thinking/pages/macroeconomic-insights-folder/the -productivity-paradox/report.pdf.

14. Bernard Hoekman, "Trade and growth—end of an era?" VoxEU, Center for Economic and Policy Research, June 20, 2015, http://www.voxeu.org/article/trade-and-growth-end-era.

15. World Bank, "Exports of Goods and Services (% of GDP)," http://data.worldbank.org/indicator/NE.EXP.GNFS.ZS, accessed August 1, 2016.

16. The Polity IV Project, "Global Trends in Governance, 1800–2014," Center for Systemic Peace, http://www.systemicpeace .org/polity/polity1.htm, accessed August 1, 2016.

17. Charles Kenny, *The Upside of Down: Why the Rise of the Rest Is Good for the West* (New York: Basic, 2013), 82.

18. Geoff Eley, *Forging Democracy: The History of the Left in Europe, 1850–2000* (New York: Oxford University Press, 2002), 17.

19. Ruy Teixeira and John Halpin, "The Progressive Tradition in American Politics," Center for American Progress, April 14, 2010, https://cdn.americanprogress.org/wp-content/uploads/issues /2010/04/pdf/progressive_traditions.pdf.

20. Jacob Hacker and Paul Pierson, *American Amnesia: How the War on Government Led Us to Forget What Made America Prosper* (New York: Simon & Schuster, 2016).

21. Donald L. Barlett and James B. Steele, *America: What Went Wrong?* (Riverside, NJ: Andrew McMeel Publishing, 1992); Hedrick Smith, *Who Stole the American Dream?* (New York: Random House, 2012); Robert D. Putnam, *Our Kids: The American Dream in Crisis* (New York: Simon & Schuster, 2015); and Tony Judt, *Ill Fares the Land* (New York: Penguin, 2010).

22. Thomas D. Snyder, ed., *120 Years of American Education: A Statistical Portrait* (Washington, DC: National Center for Education Statistics, January 1993), http://nces.ed.gov/pubs93/93442 .pdf.

23. US Bureau of the Census, "CPS Historical Time Series Tables," Table A-2, http://www.census.gov/hhes/socdemo/education /data/cps/historical/index.html, accessed August 1, 2016.

24. Pew Research Center, "The American Middle Class Is Losing Ground," Pew Research Center, December 9, 2015, http://www .pewsocialtrends.org/2015/12/09/the-american-middle-class-is -losing-ground/.

25. Anna Maria Barry-Jester, "Attitudes Toward Racism and Inequality Are Shifting," fivethirtyeight.com, June 23, 2015, http:// fivethirtyeight.com/datalab/attitudes-toward-racism-and -inequality-are-shifting/; and Gallup Organization, "Race Relations," Gallup.com, http://www.gallup.com/poll/1687/race -relations.aspx, accessed August 1, 2016.

26. Snyder, *120 Years of American Education.*

27. US Bureau of the Census, "CPS Historical Time Series Tables."

28. National Center for Education Statistics, "Undergraduate Enrollment," The Condition of Education, http://nces.ed.gov /programs/coe/indicator_cha.asp, accessed August 1, 2016.

29. National Center for Education Statistics, "Degrees conferred by sex and race," Fast Facts, https://nces.ed.gov/fastfacts/display .asp?id=72, accessed August 2, 2016.

30. Mark J. Perry, "Women earned majority of doctoral degrees in 2012 for 4th straight year, and outnumber men in grad school 141 to 100," American Enterprise Institute: AEIdeas, September 30, 2013, https://www.aei.org/publication/women-earned-majority -of-doctoral-degrees-in-2012-for-4th-straight-year-and -outnumber-men-in-grad-school-141-to-100/; Phillip Cohen, "More Women Are Doctors and Lawyers Than Ever—but Progress Is Stalling," *The Atlantic* (December 11, 2012), http://www .theatlantic.com/sexes/archive/2012/12/more-women-are -doctors-and-lawyers-than-ever-but-progress-is-stalling/266115/.

31. Tom W. Smith, "Changes in Family Values, Family Structure and Politics, 1972–2006," in Ruy Teixeira, ed., *Red, Blue and Purple America: The Future of Election Demographics* (Washington, DC: Brookings Institution Press, 2008), 147–193.

32. James Salzman, "Why Rivers No Longer Burn," *Slate,* December 10, 2012, http://www.slate.com/articles/health_and_science

/science/2012/12/clean_water_act_40th_anniversary_the
_greatest_success_in_environmental_law.html.

33. US Environmental Protection Agency, "Progress in Cleaning the Air and Improving the People's Health," Clean Air Act Overview, https://www.epa.gov/clean-air-act-overview/progress-cleaning-air-and-improving-peoples-health#pollution, accessed August 2, 2016.

34. US Geological Survey, "National Acid Precipitation Assessment Program Report to Congress: An Integrated Assessment," National Acid Precipitation Assessment Program, December 28, 2011, http://ny.water.usgs.gov/projects/NAPAP/NAPAP_2011_Report_508_Compliant.pdf.

35. Lauren Raab, "How bad was L.A.'s smog when Barack Obama went to college here?" Los Angeles Times, August 23, 2015, http://www.latimes.com/local/lanow/la-me-ln-obama-smog-20150803-htmlstory.html.

36. Author's analysis of Maddison Project historical GDP data series, http://www.ggdc.net/maddison/maddison-project/home.htm, accessed January 23, 2016.

37. Household income is not available from this survey until 1967.

38. Lawrence Mishel, Josh Bivens, Elise Gould and Heidi Shierholz, The State of Working America, 12th Edition (Ithaca, NY: ILR Press, 2012), 53–87.

39. Mishel, et al., The State of Working America, 12th Edition; Stephen J. Rose, "Was JFK Wrong? Does Rising Productivity No Longer Lead to Substantial Middle Class Income Gains?" The Information Technology & Innovation Foundation, December 2014, http://www2.itif.org/2014-rising-productivity-middle-class.pdf; Gary Burtless, "Alternative methods for measuring income and inequality," Brookings Institution, January 11, 2016, https://www.brookings.edu/on-the-record/alternative-methods-for-measuring-income-and-inequality/.

40. Authors's analysis of Congressional Budget Office income data, https://www.cbo.gov/publication/51361, accessed August 2, 2016.

41. Pew Research Center, "Pursuing the American Dream: Economic Mobility Across Generations" Pew Research Center, July,

2012, http://www.pewtrusts.org/~/media/legacy/uploadedfiles/wwwpewtrustsorg/reports/economic_mobility/pursuing americandreampdf.pdf.

42. Rose, "Was JFK Wrong?"

43. Pew Research Center, "The American Middle Class Is Losing Ground."

44. See Lane Kenworthy, *The Good Society*, chapter 6, "Shared Prosperity," July 2016, https://lanekenworthy.net/shared-prosperity /, accessed August 2, 2016; Anthony P. Carnevale and Stephen J. Rose, *The Economy Goes to College: The Hidden Promise of Higher Education in the Post-Industrial Service Economy* (Center on Education and the Workforce, Georgetown University, 2015).

45. Luxemburg Income Study data summarized in Kenworthy, *The Good Society*, Appendix to "Shared Prosperity" chapter, January 2015, https://lanekenworthy.net/shared-prosperity-additional -data/, accessed August 2, 2016.

46. Lane Kenworthy, email to author, March 24, 2016.

47. Bureau of Labor Statistics, "The Employment Situation—June 2016," BLS News Release, July 8, 2016, http://www.bls.gov /news.release/pdf/empsit.pdf, accessed August 2, 2016.

48. Doug Short, "Real Median Household Income Up Slightly in June," *Advisor Perspectives*, July 21, 2016, http://www.advisor perspectives.com/dshort/updates/Median-Household-Income -Update.

49. Debate has been vigorous about whether Obama could, in fact, have done much better, given his political constraints, both in this instance and in other actions related to the economy. See Noam Scheiber, *The Escape Artists: How Obama's Team Fumbled the Recovery* (New York: Simon & Schuster, 2012), for the best overview of his administration's actions in this area and where mistakes may have been made.

50. Alan S. Blinder and Mark Zandi, "Stimulus Worked," International Monetary Fund, Finance & Development, December, 2010, https://www.imf.org/external/pubs/ft/fandd/2010/12/pdf /Blinder.pdf.

51. His book is Michael Grunwald, *The New New Deal: The Hidden*

Story of Change in the Obama Era (New York: Simon & Schuster, 2012); the quote is from Grunwald, "Think Again: Obama's New Deal" *Foreign Policy*, August 12, 2012, http://foreignpolicy.com/2012/08/13/think-again-obamas-new-deal/.

52. Grunwald, "Think Again."

53. Harry Stein, "The Obama Health Care Legacy: More Coverage and Less Spending," Center for American Progress, March 25, 2016, https://www.americanprogress.org/issues/economy/news/2016/03/25/134074/the-obama-health-care-legacy-more-coverage-and-less-spending/.

54. Matthew Yglesias, "Dodd-Frank is Obama's most underappreciated achievement," Vox.com, July 24, 2016, http://www.vox.com/2014/7/24/5930247/financial-reform-is-working, accessed August 2, 2016; Matt O'Brien, "What Republicans and Bernie Sanders get wrong about Wall Street," Wonkblog, *Washington Post*, February 3, 2016, https://www.washingtonpost.com/news/wonk/wp/2016/02/03/what-republicans-and-bernie-sanders-both-get-wrong-about-wall-street/.

55. See, for example, Dylan Matthews, "Barack Obama is officially one of the most consequential presidents in American history," Vox.com, July 5, 2016, http://www.vox.com/2015/6/26/8849925/obama-obamacare-history-presidents, accessed August 2, 2016; Paul Krugman, "In Defense of Obama," *Rolling Stone*, October 8, 2014, http://www.rollingstone.com/politics/news/in-defense-of-obama-20141008; Michael Grunwald, "The Nation He Built," *Politico Magazine*, January/February 2016, http://www.politico.com/magazine/story/2016/01/obama-biggest-achievements-213487; Paul Glastris, Ryan Cooper and Siyu Hu, "Obama's Top 50 Accomplishments," *Washington Monthly*, March/April 2012, http://washingtonmonthly.com/magazine/marchapril-2012/obamas-top-50-accomplishments/.

56. Quoted in Matthews, "Barack Obama is officially one of the most consequential presidents in American history."

57. Manuel Funke, Moritz Schularick and Christoph Trebesch, "Going to Extremes: Politics after Financial Crisis, 1870–2014," Center for Economic Studies & Ifo Institute, CESifo Working

Paper No. 5553, October 2015, http://www.statewatch.org/news/2015/oct/financial-crises-cesifo-wp-5553.pdf.

58. The Economist, "Rose thou art sick," Briefing, *The Economist*, April 2, 2016, http://www.economist.com/news/briefing/21695887-centre-left-sharp-decline-across-europe-rose-thou-art-sick.

59. This study and other relevant literature are ably summarized in Dylan Matthews, "The great money-in-politics myth," Vox.com, February 9, 2016, http://www.vox.com/2016/2/9/10941690/campaign-finance-left, accessed August 2, 2016.

60. Tom Randall, "Wind and Solar Are Crushing Fossil Fuels," Bloomberg, April 6, 2016, http://www.bloomberg.com/news/articles/2016-04-06/wind-and-solar-are-crushing-fossil-fuels.

61. United Nations Environment Programme, "Global Trends In Renewable Energy Investment 2016," Frankfurt School of Finance & Management, 2016, http://fs-unep-centre.org/sites/default/files/publications/globaltrendsinrenewableenergyinvestment2016lowres_0.pdf.

62. Randall, "Wind and Solar Are Crushing Fossil Fuels."

63. Ramez Naam, "Is Moore's Law Really a Fair Comparison for Solar?" rameznaam.com, April 2015, http://rameznaam.com/2011/03/17/expis-moores-law-really-a-fair-comparison-for-solar/, accessed August 2, 2016.

64. See Ramez Naam, "Why Energy Storage is About to Get Big—and Cheap," rameznaam.com, April 14, 2015, http://rameznaam.com/2015/04/14/energy-storage-about-to-get-big-and-cheap/, accessed August 2, 2016; and Ramez Naam, *The Infinite Resource: The Power of Ideas on a Finite Planet* (Lebanon, NH: University Press of New England, 2013).

65. Energy analyst Michael Levi's article, "Fracking and the Climate Debate," *Democracy* (Summer 2015), http://democracyjournal.org/magazine/37/fracking-and-the-climate-debate/, is the best explication of this viewpoint. See also Michael Levi, *The Power Surge: Energy, Opportunity, and the Battle for America's Future* (New York: Oxford University Press, 2013), 20–49.

66. US Environmental Protection Agency, "Assessment of the Potential Impacts of Hydraulic Fracturing for Oil and Gas on

Drinking Water Resources: Executive Summary," Office of Research and Development, June 2015, https://www.epa.gov/sites/production/files/2015-07/documents/hf_es_erd_jun2015.pdf.

67. National Research Council, *Induced Seismicity Potential in Energy Technologies* (Washington, DC: National Academies Press, 2013); Levi, *The Power Surge*, 43–46.

68. Heartland Monitor, "Allstate/National Journal Heartland Monitor XXV Key Findings," January 2016, http://heartlandmonitor.com/wp-content/uploads/2016/01/FTI-Allstate-NJ-Heartland-Poll-XXV-Findings-Memo-Jan-11-at-4pm-ET.pdf.

CHAPTER FIVE

1. Working Party on Climate, Investment and Development, "Long-Term Economic Growth and Environmental Pressure: Reference Scenarios for Future Global Projections," Environment Directorate, Organisation for Economic Co-operation and Development, September 26, 2012, http://www.oecd.org/officialdocuments/publicdisplaydocumentpdf/?cote=ENV/EPOC/WPCID(2012)6&docLanguage=En.

2. Thomas Piketty, *Capital in the Twenty-First Century* (Cambridge, MA: Harvard University Press, 2014), 100.

3. Working Party on Climate, Investment and Development, "Long-Term Economic Growth and Environmental Pressure: Reference Scenarios for Future Global Projections."

4. This assumes that, since household income has now reached its previous peak from 2007, family income has as well.

5. Stephen J. Rose, email to author, April 29, 2016.

6. Stephen J. Rose, "The Growing Size and Incomes of the Upper Middle Class," Urban Institute Research Report, June 2016, http://www.urban.org/sites/default/files/alfresco/publication-pdfs/2000819-The-Growing-Size-and-Incomes-of-the-Upper-Middle-Class.pdf.

7. Piketty, *Capital in the Twenty-First Century*, 70–71, 313; Branko Milanovic, *Global Inequality* (Cambridge, MA: Harvard University Press, 2016), 217–222.

8. Lane Kenworthy, *Social Democratic America* (NY: Oxford University Press, 2014), 4–7.

9. Larry Summers, "Four Common Sense Ideas for Economic Growth," Capital Ideas Blog, March 1, 2016, http://www.chicagobooth.edu/capideas/blog/2016/march/four-common-sense-ideas-for-economic-growth-larry-summers.

10. American Society of Civil Engineers, "2013 Report Card for America's Infrastructure," American Society of Civil Engineers, 2013, http://www.infrastructurereportcard.org/a/documents/2013-Report-Card.pdf; and American Society of Civil Engineers, "Failure to Act: Closing the Infrastructure Investment Gap for America's Economic Future," American Society of Civil Engineers, 2016, http://www.infrastructurereportcard.org/wp-content/uploads/2016/05/2016-FTA-Report-Close-the-Gap.pdf.

11. Data in this and next paragraph from Virun Sivaram and Teryn Norris, "The Clean Energy Revolution: Fighting Climate Change With Innovation," *Foreign Affairs*, April 18, 2016, https://www.foreignaffairs.com/articles/united-states/2016-04-18/clean-energy-revolution.

12. See Thomas Piketty, "A New Deal for Europe," *The New York Review of Books*, February 25, 2016, http://www.nybooks.com/articles/2016/02/25/a-new-deal-for-europe/.

13. Milanovic, *Global Inequality*, 50–59.

14. Monty G. Marshall and Benjamin R. Cole, "Global Report 2014 Conflict, Governance, and State Fragility," Center for Systemic Peace, July 23, 2014, 24, http://www.systemicpeace.org/vlibrary/GlobalReport2014.pdf.

15. Steven Pinker, quoted in Zack Beauchamp, "5 Reasons Why 2013 Was the Best Year In Human History," *Think Progress*, December 13, 2013, http://thinkprogress.org/security/2013/12/11/3036671/2013-certainly-year-human-history/; see also Steven Pinker, *The Better Angels of Our Nature: Why Violence Has Declined* (New York: Viking, 2011).

16. Pew Research Center, "Muslim Publics Share Concerns about Extremist Groups," September 10, 2013, http://www.pewglobal.org/2013/09/10/muslim-publics-share-concerns-about

-extremist-groups/; Pew Research Center, "In nations with significant Muslim populations, much disdain for ISIS," November 17, 2015, http://www.pewresearch.org/fact-tank/2015/11/17/in-nations-with-significant-muslim-populations-much-disdain-for-isis/.

17. Author's analysis of data in Ruy Teixeira, William H. Frey and Robert Griffin, "States of Change: The Demographic Evolution of the American Electorate, 1974–2060," Center for American Progress and American Enterprise Institute, February 2015, https://cdn.americanprogress.org/wp-content/uploads/2015/02/SOC-report1.pdf; and Ruy Teixeira, John Halpin and Robert Griffin, "The Path to 270 in 2016: Can the Obama Coalition Survive?" Center for American Progress, December 2015, https://cdn.americanprogress.org/wp-content/uploads/2015/12/16133227/Pathto270_2016.pdf.

18. Ayn Rand, *Atlas Shrugged* (New York: New American Library, 1957).

19. Richard Dawkins, *The Selfish Gene* (New York: Oxford University Press, 1976).

20. Milton Friedman and Rose Friedman, *Free to Choose: A Personal Statement* (New York: Houghton Mifflin Harcourt, 1980).

21. See, for example, Elliot Sober and David Sloan Wilson, *Unto Others: The Evolution and Psychology of Unselfish Behavior* (Cambridge, MA: Harvard University Press, 1998); Martin Nowak with Roger Highfield, *SuperCooperators: Altruism, Evolution and Why We Need Each Other to Succeed* (New York: Free Press, 2011); and Edward O. Wilson, *The Social Conquest of Earth* (New York: Norton, 2012).

22. These results and others are summarized in great detail in Alexander J. Field, *Altruistically Inclined?: The Behavioral Sciences, Evolutionary Theory and the Origins of Reciprocity* (Ann Arbor, MI: University of Michigan Press, 2001), 29–92; and Samuel Bowles and Herbert Gintis, *A Cooperative Species: Human Reciprocity and Its Evolution* (Princeton, NJ: Princeton University Press, 2011).

23. Richard H. Thaler and Cass R. Sunstein, *Nudge: Improving Decisions About Health, Wealth, and Happiness* (New York:

Penguin, 2009); Daniel Kahneman, *Thinking, Fast and Slow* (New York: Farrar, Straus and Giroux, 2011).

24. For an elegant summary of the crisis in mainstream economics, see John Cassidy, *How Markets Fail: The Logic of Economic Calamities* (New York: Farrar, Straus and Giroux, 2009).

25. Charles Kenny, *The Upside of Down: Why the Rise of the Rest Is Good for the West* (New York: Basic, 2013).

INDEX